Building a Ministry of
Comfort and Compassion

Building a Ministry of Comfort and Compassion

◆

A Young Widow's Journey

Elaine Cook

iUniverse, Inc.
New York Lincoln Shanghai

Building a Ministry of Comfort and Compassion
A Young Widow's Journey

Copyright © 2005 by Elaine K. Cook

iUniverse books may be ordered through booksellers or by contacting:

iUniverse
2021 Pine Lake Road, Suite 100
Lincoln, NE 68512
www.iuniverse.com
1-800-Authors (1-800-288-4677)

ISBN-13: 978-0-595-35411-5 (pbk)
ISBN-13: 978-0-595-67216-5 (cloth)
ISBN-13: 978-0-595-79907-7 (ebk)
ISBN-10: 0-595-35411-4 (pbk)
ISBN-10: 0-595-67216-7 (cloth)
ISBN-10: 0-595-79907-8 (ebk)

Printed in the United States of America

I dedicate this book in loving memory of my late husband, Stan, and for all of the other husbands of the widows I have had the pleasure and honor to serve.

Contents

Acknowledgments

I would like to thank all the friends and widows who gave me practical and emotional support during my own journey into and through widowhood. I would like to specifically thank my son, Tyler, for believing in me during our journey, for being there in constant support for all that God has given me in the way of vision, and for sacrificing by allowing me to minister to so many widows, when perhaps I should have been at home with him more.

I would like to extend my heartfelt thanks to my wonderful Sunday—school class. I cannot mention all of your names, but you know who you are. You loved and prayed me through a time of complete shock and despair for Tyler and me. Thank you for loving me and becoming my sisters in Christ. By knowing you and being a recipient of your never-ending compassion, I have grown in the Lord, and I share it with many others. Where would I be without you? I praise God for each and every one of you.

I would also like to thank my church family for taking Tyler and me in and welcoming us with no questions asked. Your prayers and efforts have never gone unnoticed or unappreciated. I will never know what roles many of you played, but God does, and may each of you have a special place in eternity for coming to the aid of this widow and orphan, as you were commanded to do in Scripture.

Lord, I thank you from the bottom of my heart for all that I have learned and for the blessings I have received. I have gone through times of being angry and giving up, but you remain faithful, and you love and guide me regardless of where I stand. You have not forsaken me, and I thank you for the trials I have gone through in order to have a better relationship with you, and for the glory of your kingdom.

And to my dear friend, Peggy: thank you for constantly believing in me and encouraging me to reach out and continue what God has laid upon my heart. I still don't know sometimes why God felt it be so amusing to pair the two of us up, but I praise God for your wonderful friendship and for being the sister I never had.

I cannot complete my thank-yous without including a big hug for you, Larry. Thank you for believing in me and constantly sacrificing in order that many women could be ministered to. I am so thankful that God brought you into our lives and for you having such a big heart. I love you.

Prologue

This book is in response to the hundreds of women that I have had the privilege to meet on their journeys through widowhood. It is not an easy journey, and I have met ladies from all walks of life. I have learned so much from these ladies and their stories of their journeys. Some are very enlightening, some are sad, and some show the strength of our Lord Jesus Christ in how they have overcome their difficulties.

I have met with women who have lost their husbands suddenly in tragic accidents and because of heart attacks. I have met with women who had to watch their husbands suffer for long periods of time with agonizing illnesses. I have met with women whose husbands have fought in wars and lost their lives while defending their country. I have met with women whose husbands have taken their own lives or have been murdered. I have met with women whose husbands died at the hands of terrorists.

One thing I know for sure: it does not matter how our husbands died; we struggle in our own ways, and the tragedy remains and the survivors must pick up their broken hearts and try to make sense of a new life they were not looking for.

Young widows often feel that they have been robbed of their futures, robbed of growing old with their husbands. For older widows, it is often a feeling of what is left for them to do.

I hope this book helps widows of all walks of life and encourages family members, friends, and ministers by providing suggestions on how to help widows. This book is simply a reflection of what God has done in the life of this young widow and how I have gone beyond that in being obedient to the call to help others by founding the ministry called Widow2Widow™, Inc.

1

The Beginning of the Journey

It was a cold morning, January 10, 2000, when I threw a bag into the car and worried about the telephone call I had just received. It was approximately 1:30 A.M, and I looked at the gas gauge and realized the light was on, indicating that my husband, Stan, once again had not filled up the car. I recalled how many times I had asked him to keep gas in his vehicle in case of emergencies. In our years together, there had been numerous times we had run out of gas. This was his car, and I could not stand driving it. It was a four-cylinder and a manual, and now I had to drive it, hoping I wouldn't have to stop on a hill and need to get started again. I arrived at a gas station right before the entrance onto the interstate and realized I had only two dollars in change in my purse. Earlier that evening, I had given Stan the last of my cash when he and our eleven-year-old son, Tyler, had headed for our new home in Nashville.

I finally got onto the interstate with so many memories filling my mind and my heart, and I thought about every word we'd shared just moments before when they had arrived in Nashville just a few hours earlier. I tried to make sense of the conversation that we'd had.

The day before had been such a wonderful day; it's one that I still cherish. We had been in the process of getting the big items in the house packed for our move to Nashville. Stan and Tyler were leaving that evening to make their final trip. I was staying behind to work out all of the final arrangements with the movers that were to come on Thursday, so we could all be together again in one house on Friday. We had been apart for six weeks and were looking forward to being a family again.

That day we'd worked so hard, and then, a few hours before Stan and Tyler were to leave on their trip, Stan had taken a nap on the couch and laid his head in my lap. He loved it when I would run my fingers through his hair and massage his temples. I remember looking down at him; he had been dozing off with a smile on his face, and every once in a while, he had looked up at me and just grinned. Oh, that handsome grin of his. I had dozed off with him, and neither of us had moved until it was time to get up.

It had come time to see them off. Stan, Tyler, and Rocky (our *labrador*/Australian shepherd) had piled into the van after we'd crammed as much stuff as possible in, hoping that they would have everything they would need for the week until the movers and I arrived on Friday. We'd had our family hug, and I had kissed them both good-bye. Tyler had been so excited to spend some time alone with his dad and to start his new school in two days. And Stan couldn't wait until the family could be together.

I had stood out in the street and waved until they were completely out of sight. Then I had walked back into the house and begun to pack until I had been able to get it all done and make final preparations before going to bed. I had needed to get up early the next morning to go in to work and get things lined up for my trip to Nashville on Friday.

About six hours later, I had received a call from our home in the Nashville area. Stan and Tyler had arrived at their final destination. It had been about 11:00 PM, and they had been very tired from all of the traveling and packing. Stan had kept talking and talking, saying he was anxious for Friday to arrive so that we could all be home together. He reassured me that our lives would be wonderful in Tennessee (we had moved so often and lived in many states).

It had been six weeks since he had begun his new job, and he loved what he was doing. He was finally making enough money that I could take a lower-paying job. (I would start the next week.) Stan had turned his conversation to how much he'd enjoyed his trip with Tyler and how much our son had changed in those weeks. Tyler had found a new George Strait song called "My Best Friend," and he would not let Stan get out of the van until he had heard it all the way through. Stan would do a little thing with his nose when he would get emotional, and I could picture him doing that when he talked about his love for our son and how proud he was to be his dad. It was such an exciting and joyful conversation.

I had been very excited as he was talking. I was so in love with him, and I'd told him how much I loved him. That was to be the last conversation I was to have with my sweet husband, and I praise God. It was a wonderful display of love and affection, and it will last me a lifetime.

I finished packing for the evening and fell asleep on the couch. I woke up having what turned out to be the first of many panic attacks, and I could not understand what was wrong. My chest was hurting, and I was clammy and sweaty. This was something I had never experienced before. Suddenly, I heard my husband tell me everything was going to be okay and that he loved me. At that very moment, the phone rang. It was 1:15 AM, and I jumped up and looked at the caller ID. I heaved a huge sigh of relief, because it was the number of our home in Nashville. I picked up the phone and asked what was wrong. The voice on the other end was not my husband's but a police officer's, telling me that my son had called 911 and that the paramedics were working on my husband.

I was in complete shock, and I felt as though I had left my body. I was hearing what the officer was saying, but how could that be my Stan he was referring to? Surely they had the wrong number. Please, let this not be true! The officer put Tyler on the phone, and Tyler was so brave. He said that Daddy was going to be okay and assured me he could still hear him breathing. I told him to do just what the officers told him to do and said that I loved him and would be there as soon as I could. Tyler told me to be careful and that he loved me. Then the officer got back on the phone and said that I needed to get there as fast as I could: if I got stopped by any law enforcement, I was to give the officer his cell phone number. He said not to worry about Tyler because they would make sure he was in good hands. I just needed to get there—and fast.

I had not unpacked from my trip the day before, so I threw that bag in the car, secured the house, and was on my way.

Throughout the several-hour drive, I just kept praying. I was praying for God to please take care of my son. (In my heart, I just knew that my beloved husband would not survive whatever it was.) There was no one I could call to be there with Tyler, to comfort him and to keep him from being afraid. I had to believe that God would care for him and provide for him. I prayed that God wouldn't be upset with me for not praying and being obedient until I needed something from him in desperation.

As I approached Nashville, the officer called my cell phone to ask where I was and gave me directions to the hospital. Since I had only come on the weekends, I only knew how to get to our home in Nashville. I was completely unaware of everything else. As I got to the hospital, my legs and arms felt very heavy and I could hardly move. I was not sure what was facing me inside those doors, but I felt that I knew. It was more frightening than I ever could have imagined.

I walked up and was greeted by hospital staff who took me into a little room. I asked to see my son before I sat down. He was in another room, sleeping. I stood there, not knowing what he had been through that night. I watched him sleep, kissed him on the forehead, caressed his hair, and thanked God for taking care of him.

I went back to the little room. I was frightened because the last time I had been taken to a room like this had been in Houston, Texas, on January 8, 1992, when I had been told that my daddy had suffered a massive heart attack. He had not survived. I asked the nurses if my husband had survived, and they just kept telling me that the doctor would be in shortly. Finally, after what seemed like an eternity (but what was probably only about ten minutes), the doctor came in, took my hand, and said that my husband (at the age of forty-five) had suffered a massive heart attack. He told me that it was so severe that even if he had been in the hospital, they would not have been able to save him.

He proceeded to tell me that there was something else I needed to know. The doctor said that my husband had died in the arms of our eleven-year-old son, and Tyler had not been told that he had died. What Tyler had heard when he told me not to worry were the last noises a body makes after someone has passed on. The paramedics hadn't been keeping him from having a heart attack; they had been trying to revive him after one.

The doctor asked if there was anyone they could call. I told him that we did not know one soul in Tennessee—that we were completely alone. I did not even have the number of my husband's workplace; I only had his direct line. I told him the name of the company and asked that they let them know what happened. I also asked them to call my office in Little Rock.

I asked to see my husband, and they said it would take a few moments for them to place him in another room. I waited and waited, and then a couple of nurses walked with me down a long corridor. You know, in the movies, how a hallway can seem to get longer and longer, and you feel as if you will never get to its end? It happens in real life as well. With each step I took, the doors seemed to get farther and farther away.

We finally made it. Before they opened the door, the nurse said that they could not remove the equipment from his mouth and that I could not touch him. As I walked over to him, trying to absorb what had happened, the other nurse whispered in my ear, telling me it was okay if I wanted to touch Stan's hair. I stood there—remembering that less than twenty-four hours before his head had been in my lap and I had been running my fingers through it. He had smiled at me.

When I looked at him, my legs began to give out because I had hoped they had the wrong person. I had hoped my husband was waiting for me in another part of the hospital. But as I got closer, I could not believe that this lifeless body lying on this cold table was my beloved husband of almost fourteen years. Oh, how much we had shared together. Why couldn't he be here to help me through this too? Oh, God, why couldn't he just be looking up at me and smiling his gentle smile and telling me it was all going to be okay? Why couldn't he tell me this was not happening? How come my future was so uncertain? Why? Why at this point in our lives was this happening? Why was Tyler forced to go through his teenage years without his dad—his best friend?

I took a deep breath and forced myself to walk away, and then I found myself having to find the words to explain to my son what had happened. As I walked away, I was completely in disbelief. What was I going to tell Tyler? Rage came up in me, and then tears welled up—but why couldn't I release any of them? I felt that I needed to be strong for Tyler. All we had now was each other, and I could not let him see me fall apart—not now!

When I was growing up, I was never allowed to show emotion. I was expected to be strong and to hold my head up high. How was I going to get through this without Stan? We'd always had each other to lean on in times of crisis. When we had buried Justin, our second son, Stan's mother, and my daddy, we were always there to support each other during these difficult times. We'd had each other to lean upon. When our son had died, we had given up our faith in God. So much had happened to us that year, and we had been so young.

But now I was thirty-seven years old and suddenly a widow and single mom. And now I was faced with having a family meeting with my son—just the two of us—not the three of us. How was I going to be able to tell Tyler what had happened?

I walked into the room where my son was asleep. I asked the nurses and the doctor and everyone to let me have this time with Tyler alone. I sat him up, put his head in my lap, and caressed his hair until he woke up. I found it ironic that until a couple of years before this life-changing incident, Tyler had been the carbon copy of his daddy—same hair, same everything. For the first time since then, I truly saw his face. I realized how much he had begun to look like me. I was amused at how God prepares in the mightiest of ways. Tyler asked me how his daddy was. He had the sweetest smile and the face of innocence.

I got down on my knees and looked him in the eye. Suddenly the words that I needed to share with him came. His best friend hadn't made it. I will never forget the look Tyler had in his eyes as he tried hard to comprehend what I had told him. Tyler shouted—saying that Daddy had been breathing when they had taken him away—what had they done to him? All I could do was to take my son in my arms, hold him, and tell him how brave he had been. At the same time, I wondered just what he had gone through that night.

The chaplain came in and talked with us for a few moments. No one could understand that we had no one they could call for us. The officers that had been the first to respond to Tyler's 911 emergency call came by and told me some of what Tyler had shared with them about the events of the evening. They had said how brave he truly was and how they admired the strength that was within him.

I was told (and later Tyler confirmed) that shortly after our final conversation that night, Stan had reached up to get some aspirin. The video game was hooked up to the television so that Tyler would have something to occupy his time. Tyler had heard a noise, and aspirin had rolled all over the floor. Stan had collapsed. He had told Tyler he was just tired and needed to lie there for a little while—to go back and play. Tyler had done as his dad had asked and continued to play video games. Tyler said that after a while he had gone to check on Stan and that Stan had been unable to move. At the time, Stan had still been able to speak, and he'd told Tyler how proud he was to have him as his son. Tyler had wanted to call me, and Stan had said no; he did not want to worry me.

I do not believe that Stan knew what was happening to him. Tyler had let him rest some more, and, when Stan did not respond to him, Tyler had gone over to him, put Stan's head in his lap, told his daddy how much he loved him, and caressed his hair. He had wanted to call me, but Stan had insisted that he not call. It could not have been much longer after that when Tyler had called 911. Stan had begun to foam at the mouth, and Tyler had continued to hold his daddy, who had been unable to speak at that point. Tyler had kept telling him how much he loved him. All Stan had been able to manage as Tyler was talking was to pat Tyler's knee. I later told Tyler that he was blessed to have been there for his daddy, and that his daddy was also blessed to have been able to look up at his sweet face—the final thing he was to see—which must have given him peace. When I told Tyler this, it seemed to make him a little less frightened about what was going on and how much our lives were about to change.

I gathered up Tyler's things and signed whatever papers I was supposed to sign. I gathered up what belonged to Stan, including his torn shirt. They asked what funeral home we wanted to use. I just looked at them and reminded them that I had no clue about anything around there and just picked one off the list. How was I supposed to make these kinds of decisions in a place I was not familiar with, with people I did not know?

The police told me that the house was unlocked because they had been unable to find the keys and that they had a police car patrolling the area every few minutes. I asked about our dog, Rocky, and the officer said that someone was checking on him and feeding him until we were able to get to the house. These were the things on my mind that I could think about. I could not think of all the things I needed to do—all the things I needed to do *alone*.

The officers had to give me directions to our home because I did not know where we were. Tyler and I walked out to Stan's car and just sat there, numb and in shock. No emotion was expressed. I didn't even know what I was supposed to feel, or if I even wanted to feel anything.

Tyler asked me what we were going to do. I told him I did not know but that we would get to the house and make some phone calls and see. All I could think about was how empty I felt. I was in shock and denial. I knew Stan was dead and would not be able to be there with us, but I could not believe what had truly happened.

We drove up to the house, and there was Rocky. He was such a wonderful and sweet dog, and he knew there was something wrong. We petted him, played with him, and made sure he had all he needed.

We walked into the house, and there were all of the remnants of what had happened under that roof just hours before. The hardwood floors were scuffed up, paper was lying on the floor from the equipment the paramedics had used, and aspirin was all over the breakfast nook. I went outside to catch my breath and noticed that the van had not been unloaded; it still contained all of the things that Stan and Tyler had brought with them.

Tyler asked me again what we were going to do. I looked across the living room in disbelief, and all that was there was a television, a bar stool, games, etc. The house was empty because all of our furniture and belongings were in another state, in a house that I needed to be out of by Thursday, and this was *still* Monday morning.

We sat down on the hearth, staring at the marks on the floor and the paper left behind by the paramedics. I told my son that we were just going to have to pray about what to do, because I didn't know. No one had ever prepared me for the idea that I could become a single mom in the blink of an eye. The word *widow* had never been in my vocabulary, except to describe my mother, my grandmother, and other older ladies.

When tragedy struck, Stan had always been there. I sat there and remembered the time I had been pregnant with our second child. Tyler had been just fourteen months old when I had gotten the news that our second child was not going to live. In July 1989, I was six months pregnant, and we had gone to find out what sex the baby was. During the sonogram it had been discovered that the baby had a problem. As we sat across the desk from the doctor, he had begun to explain that the baby had a birth defect, one so rare that only one in every ten thousand babies was born with it. He called it anencephaly and proceeded to give us options. As he was describing our options in detail and offering us no hope whatsoever, I had felt as if I had left my body because I had been able to see Stan and myself sitting across from the doctor and the look of horror on Stan's face. It had seemed as if I were sitting behind us—a bystander, dissociated. We had walked out of that office unspeaking. Stan had taken my hand and begun to weep like I had never seen him weep before.

This was the hardest thing for us to go through together at the time, and our faith in God diminished. We were living in Phoenix, Arizona, and all of our family lived in Texas. How could God allow a young couple to be faced with these decisions and crush all hope?

I carried our child for another six weeks. I had the option to abort the pregnancy because it was believed the baby would not be born alive. But while I carried him, he was healthy, and he kicked my insides out. He even had the hiccups, just like his big brother had when I carried him. So we could not make the decision to abort, even with the fear that this pregnancy could cause me harm. I had gained over fifty pounds in one week because of the amniotic fluid, which was what had caused the doctor to become alarmed in the first place. We knew there was no hope, but I wanted to share in his life as much as we could and for however long we would have him. August 29, 1989, was one of the darkest moments of our married life. It was also the point where we began to lose our faith in God and place it within ourselves because we could not understand why something like this could happen and we felt that we could only depend on one another in all things.

Our son Justin was born alive, and he died in my arms forty-five minutes after he was born. Justin was a premature baby, and because no one expected him to be born alive, they had not prepared us for what he would look like. They had put a cap on his head, and his skin was so purple, and he was so tiny. I removed the cap to see that his skull had not fully developed and that his brain was exposed. But my sweet son was breathing, and I was trying to comprehend what was going to happen. Justin was one of the record few to be born alive with this birth defect. Anencephaly is when the spinal cord does not develop, so his brain was exposed, which explained the knit cap he was wearing. All of his fingers and toes were there, and I just held him. When I saw he was struggling, I handed Justin to Stan, so he could tell his son good-bye.

Stan tried to be strong and gave Justin back to me, because he just could not handle it. I held Justin, talked to him, and loved him. Stan would not release Justin's hand. Within moments, the life had exited his body. I thought it was such a precious thing to bring him into this world and to hold him as he drifted out, regardless of how long it lasted.

For a long time I questioned why I had to lose my son, and it was not until Stan's death that I realized that Justin would be in heaven to welcome his grandparents and to welcome his daddy—in a body that was not defective and suffering. It took me a long time to accept that.

It also took me a long time to accept Jesus back into my life. He didn't cause my baby's death or the death of my husband. He did not save them either, but he allowed it to happen so I would rely on him like never before. I gave up on him so many years ago—concentrating on my husband and having faith only in our lives together—but God never gave up on us. Oh, how thankful I am today for his faithfulness to his straying children.

We had not done much praying. As Tyler and I sat on the hearth, I looked across the room and recalled a time a couple of weeks earlier when we had stood there for the first time. Stan had found this house for us to rent because we were unsure about where we wanted to buy a house. I recalled our conversation with the landlords. They had asked if we went to church, and I had said no, that we gave up years ago. But Stan had told them we were going to be attending the church right over there. Over there was a Baptist church that could be seen from the front lawn. I had looked up at him and asked him if he was nuts. His comment had been that we were starting a new life in Tennessee, and it was time to get back to church and have that be a part of Tyler's life. I had been blown away by him standing firm to this new commitment. I had never been good at being the submissive wife.

Then, suddenly, I realized how alone Tyler and I were. I began to make phone calls. I called my office in Little Rock, and they said the hospital had called and told me not to worry about a thing. I spoke to my boss and asked if she could give me a five-hundred-dollar advance and deposit it into my bank account that day because I did not know what expenses I would have until I returned. I called my uncle. I called Stan's cousin, who is a preacher in Texas. I called my best friend in Texas, and I can still recall her words. She screamed out, "Oh, God, no!" It dawned on me that I hadn't cried yet. What was wrong with me? Why couldn't I show any emotion?

Tyler sat with me as I prayed silently; I turned to him and held him, trying to figure out what to do next. My son had been through so much. How could he be comforting me? Wasn't it my job to comfort him?

I called the landlords and asked them to please not do anything with the deposit check because I was not going to be able to afford the house. They were sweet and said not to worry about anything right now. I remember telling them that the paramedics had scuffed up the wooden floor where they had worked on

Stan, and I did not know how to get it cleaned up. Again, they said not to worry about it. I told them I did not know how to do some things without Stan, and they again said not to worry about it and tried to assure me that everything was going to be okay.

The phone rang, and it was Stan's company. They told me that if Tyler and I wanted to continue to make our move here, they would pay for everything. Then Stan's cousin, the preacher, called. Bobby said he would be out on a flight that night, and he would help us make the arrangements and do what was necessary. I told him that I did not know where the airport was to pick him up, but that we would get there.

Then I had to make a call to my mother. Mother was in a nursing home in Nevada and unable to be at the funeral, but because of her mental capacity, I knew I could not handle her being there. I asked to speak to her nurse and asked her to tell Mother about what had happened because I just could not talk to her right then. I knew that if I heard her voice I would lose it, and I just could not do that. There were too many things to be done.

A neighbor came by and said the landlords had called her, and she offered what help she could. She and her husband were members of the church that Stan had said we were going to be attending. Evidently, Charlotte called the church: later in the day, Gayle, who was the family life minister at the time, came to visit. I do not recall much of what she had to say, but I do recall her soft voice and gentle spirit, and how comforting she was.

The next call I made was to the funeral home, and I set up an appointment. At the time I did not know the owners were also members of the church that Stan had said we would be attending. I can see now how God was very much present in our lives.

Later in the day, I went by the funeral home and made the arrangements to have Stan cremated. After experiencing so much death in our life together, Stan and I believed that there was just too much cost involved in being laid to rest in the ground. We both wanted to be cremated because it was easier on the surviving spouse. It seemed like it would be giving the earth something back, instead of taking from it.

When we returned from the funeral home, I called a dear friend of mine, Nadine. Nadine had been my fifth-grade teacher, and she was very instrumental in the introduction of Jesus Christ into my life many years earlier. We had stayed in touch all of these years. Nadine prayed with me over the phone, and she shared the Scripture, Ecclesiastes 1:18 (NIV): "For with much wisdom comes much sorrow; the more knowledge, the more grief."

Nadine also shared something else with me that day. She told me about a gift she had always believed I had. She told me to begin keeping a journal, because she knew that one day there would be a story to tell. Nadine knew of the hardships I'd had in life and was always an encouraging force.

I could not figure out what my feelings were, much less write them down, so I kept things in my day planner. I marked the days in red that were bad days—and, in the beginning, they were all bad days. But after a while I got tired of seeing nothing but red, so I tried to find at least one blessing per day. If I found one, I would write it down in the planner and then highlight it in yellow. Over time, I began to find a lot of blessings, like the fact that I was able to get out of bed that morning or that I saw Tyler smile—just anything. My planner began to show fewer red days when I discovered even the smallest of blessings, and instead it showed a whole lot of yellow days.

Later that evening, after many phone calls, we found our way to the airport and walked up just as Bobby was getting off the plane. I had never paid attention to how much alike Bobby and Stan looked, and I went as white as a sheet when I saw his face. He just hugged both of us, and I never wanted him to let us go. I was comforted more than I ever would have imagined by having Bobby there with us. I am a very independent person, but I felt as if I could not be trusted to make even the smallest decision. All of this had happened so fast. My life was completely and totally upside down and out of control, and I was wishing it was nonexistent.

We went out for dinner, and I realized I had not eaten since the day before. I hadn't even thought about needing to eat, since there was no food at the house. I had taken Tyler to Burger King or something, but I had not even given one thought about myself because I was so sick to my stomach with all that was going on.

Bobby told us, over dinner, that if we wanted to move back to Texas, he would help us get there. My thoughts were about how easy it would be to move back to our home state of Texas and be comforted, but Tyler and I looked at one another. We both just felt that there was a reason we were in Nashville, and we wanted to give it some time.

The next morning I called Stan's office and told them we had decided to stay and that I was leaving on Wednesday to go back to Little Rock to meet the movers on Thursday morning.

Tyler and I needed to go and get him registered for his new middle school. This was something Stan was supposed to have taken care of. There were so many things—I was about to find out—that Stan was supposed to handle, and either he did not see the importance or his life ended too suddenly to get them done. I had to go through all of his things, including his briefcase, in order to find Tyler's previous school records.

Tyler had been enrolled in a small private Christian school, and now he was going to a public middle school. The thought scared me, along with so many other things. We arrived, and I explained the situation to the school officials. They took care of us and got it all handled without delay. Tyler was not able to start that day; it would be the following Monday before he would begin his new season in the school year.

We went back to the funeral home on Tuesday morning so Bobby could help me. The people at the funeral home wanted to know whether we wanted a memorial there, or whether they should ship Stan's body back to Texas. I had already given it much thought, and one of the first decisions I was to make alone followed. I said no, we did not know anyone in Tennessee, but I couldn't afford to go back to Texas for all of this because I was to start my new job the next week.

Bobby suggested that we have a memorial with the three of us. Because of my visit with them the day before, I had brought some clothes that Stan had packed. Even though he was to be cremated, they were to dress him and place him in a makeshift casket until our memorial was over. No one ever tells you these things. Where was the handbook when I got married that explained the possibility of widowhood to young brides?

Bobby helped me to unload the van filled with out belongings that Stan had driven back. Then, because of a problem with the van, Bobby took it to have it checked out, and Tyler and I were still trying to make sense of some things. I went and lay down on a couple of cots Stan had put up, and it dawned on me that I had not slept in two days. Again, there were just so many things to be done, and I didn't have anyone to rely upon to handle them.

Bobby was there, but I knew my time alone was about to begin. It was hard because I did not have any friends or family there to comfort me and to assure me that I would get through this. Yet, in the back of my mind, I felt a presence that brought some sort of peace—when I would allow it.

I could not sleep. I kept tossing and turning and found myself in a puddle of tears that I finally allowed myself to shed because Bobby was taking care of Tyler so I could rest. I had not really given myself permission to cry. I was still afraid that if I began, there would be no end, so I got up and started going through the mail. Stan had had the mail forwarded, and I had been teaching him how to pay the bills since he was going to be taking on this responsibility.

What I found confirmed my worst fears. There were things that Stan had not paid—like life insurance. I also found out that he needed to be on his job three more weeks before his medical and life benefits kicked in. Things were not looking good financially, but I could not make any calls to confirm anything until later in the week, since we had everything packed up for the movers. It was another stress, on top of everything else.

On Tuesday afternoon, we met at the funeral home for our family memorial to Stan. I went into the room first to spend some time alone with him, and the force of what was happening was beginning to build up within me. I panicked again, and this time I did not hear Stan's voice telling me everything was going to be okay.

My heart began to race, and the pain in my chest was almost unbearable. I took deep breaths and looked at my sweet husband. After a little while, Bobby brought Tyler into the room. We sat down on the couch, and Bobby explained to Tyler about death and heaven and eternity. He explained it in such a special way for my son, and yet I do not know how much of it Tyler understood. But Tyler walked up to where his daddy lay and just stood there, looking at him. I walked up to him and put my arms around him, and Tyler made the comment that it did not look like his daddy. Bobby proceeded to tell him about the spirit leaving his body and how we would carry his memory in our hearts.

Bobby said his good-byes and took Tyler into another room so I could spend time with my best friend, my lover, my confidant, my protector, and my husband for the last time. I stood beside him, stroking his hair (as he always enjoyed me doing) and trying to fix it to look how he usually wore it. I touched his clothes and held his face, which, of course, was cold, but it was his. But I knew it would be the last time I would ever see him again, at least in that body. I leaned over, kissed him, and began to cry. Again, I was afraid that if I cried I would not be able to stop, so I kept beating myself up—telling myself that crying was not the thing to do. It was building up inside me, but I did not want Tyler to see me cry, so I stayed until I was able to control it. I wiped away my tears, held my husband's hand once more, and said I loved him. I knew that I needed to say good-bye, but that would mean that it was final. I was not ready to finalize my relationship with him. It was not until a long while later that I realized that saying good-bye may have finalized my relationship as Stan's wife, but it also began a whole new journey as I fell into the loving arms of our Heavenly Father.

I went out to join Tyler and Bobby and to face a new life that I did not want. I wanted my life back, with Stan at my side comforting me. I wanted my life back, with all of the happiness that we'd had in our marriage. I wanted him to lie down with me at night; I wanted to feel him breathing next to me; I wanted him to put his arms around me. I wanted the intimacy that only he and I had shared as husband and wife. I wanted him. I was thirty-seven years old, suddenly a single mom, and what was that *W* word? *Widow?* Can someone so young be such a word?

We drove off, and all of us were silent. What words could be expressed? I felt so empty and so alone and so overwhelmed. I was confused and fearful and in such pain. I longed to be able to talk to someone who might have an understanding of what I was going through. I needed for someone to take control of my life because everything was so out of control.

The next morning Bobby and I drove all over Nashville trying to find Stan's office so I could clean out his desk and gather the check so I could pay the movers. We got there, and, for the first time, I was faced with people who didn't know what to say. They looked at me, feeling sorry for me. They just did not know what to say or do.

Going through Stan's things was more difficult than I could have imagined, but, if I had ever doubted the love he had for his family, my doubts were quickly extinguished. Among the items in his desk were pictures of Tyler and me, artwork that Tyler had specially made for his daddy, and cards that I used to leave in his suitcase every time we were apart.

There had never been a day when we hadn't spoken; even when Stan had traveled around the world, he'd made the point to call home: whatever the cost. This was the first time I was faced with not hearing his voice, so looking at his personal things he kept at work brought comfort to me because they expressed his love for us when he couldn't be with us. His love was still surrounding me in a way that you would not understand unless you have experienced this kind of loss.

We left and headed home so that we could pack up and head out to Little Rock so Bobby could catch a plane there—and so Tyler and I could go to the house and get things ready for the final move.

We got to Little Rock, and Bobby kept insisting he would stay with us until we got settled. I told him that we appreciated his love and support, but he had his family to return to, as well as a congregation that needed him. Once we had dropped Bobby off at the airport so he could catch his flight back to Dallas, Tyler and I drove to my office in downtown Little Rock to clear out my desk. Once again, we were bombarded with hugs and looks—people feeling sorry for us and the ones that did not know what to say or do.

What I found interesting as I was cleaning out my things was that if I had been the one to go first, what would there have been on my desk that would have brought comfort to Stan and Tyler as they were forced into this task? I have been careful every day since then about what legacy I am leaving for my family. What will my death say about the life I shared on this earth? Not the material things, but the spiritual, and acts of love and kindness.

On the way to the house, we stopped by the karate studio Tyler had been going to for a few months; he loved his instructor. I explained to his instructor what had happened two days before, and he took Tyler aside and hugged him and cried with him. I was never so touched in all of my life as I was at that moment, seeing how this sweet man loved him and became his friend, not just his instructor.

Then the dreaded moment came. It came time to go to the house and figure more things out. The thought of being in that house scared me because it was the last place we three had been a family.

We drove up to our home, and our neighbor ran over as we got out of the van, bombarding me with questions about where had I been, because she had missed me. I had left in the middle of the night two days before, and I hadn't called to let them know what had happened. We sat on the front porch, and she began to cry as I told her what had unfolded over the past forty-eight hours. Maxine helped with Tyler while I worked in the house, packing, cleaning, and returning phone calls.

At one point the phone rang, and it was the Little Rock landlords. They wanted a full month's rent, and I told them that we had sent them a letter as per our lease agreement, giving plenty of notice. They became very ugly and wanted to talk to Stan. I sat there listening to this rudeness and blurted out that Stan was dead. The man did not believe me and wanted the name of the funeral home. So I gave it to him and told him that the movers would be there the next day and he could come by if he wanted, but I did not see the point. I never heard from them again.

This was the first of many occasions that I became angry. I was not sure if I was mad at God because of the loss of our son, mad at Stan for not taking care of himself, or mad at myself for being angry and not being strong.

I could not face the idea of spending the night in that house, so Tyler and I spent the night at a hotel. The next morning, which was Thursday, we loaded the van with what we could, and the movers loaded everything else. Leaving that house wasn't supposed to be so hard. It was supposed to be a time of joy, to be able to leave there and move on to a new life in Nashville. What I could not comprehend was that the new life was going to happen in Nashville; it just was not going to be with Stan.

Tyler and I arrived back in Nashville late on Thursday night, and again we were greeted by Tyler's dog, Rocky. He was so glad to see us. I do not know how animals know things, but Rocky seemed to know everything and would immediately run up to us and lie at our feet and comfort us in special ways. He was such a smart dog. We figured Rocky must have been raised by cats because he knew how to open doors and gates with his paws. He amused us in the smallest of ways during that time. I realized later on that God found those small moments to bring us comfort and joy.

On Friday morning, I began to go through some papers that had I kept out of the moving truck and began to make phone calls. My worst fears were coming to light. Stan had let every insurance policy lapse because he had not seen the importance of them and because he did not know how to pay bills well. I would soon face many other issues because of his lack of ability.

I also realized it had been two weeks since I was supposed to have my period, and I spent the next three months horrified that I was thirty-seven years old, a widowed, single mother, in a new state, and possibly pregnant. But praise be to God, our Father. Three months later it was confirmed that I was not pregnant. I am not sure how I would have handled that situation. After all, there are many women who are faced with much more and have to face it alone.

2

How God Uses Others

Gayle from the church came by again and dropped off sandwiches for Tyler and me, as well as for the movers. She spent some time with me, and though I do not recall our conversation, I was comforted by her very presence—her soft voice and her gentle heart. She invited Tyler to come to the church that night for an "un-birthday party" (this had to be a Tennessee thing). He was excited to be invited, and I told her (after I got the look from his eager eyes) that he would be there, but there was no way I could stay.

The time came to get Tyler to the church, and as we were about to walk in, another panic attack came over me. I had to take deep breaths, and finally I built up enough courage to go into a room filled with strangers. They were all so sweet. They had everything ready for Tyler's arrival, and once I knew he was okay, I eased my way out of there and headed home.

I cried and I cried like I had never cried before in my life. It was the first time Tyler and I had been apart from one another for more than a few moments, and I had to release everything that was pent up inside of me, before I absolutely burst.

A few hours later, I arrived at the church and stood in the background, trying not to be noticed. I watched my son fit in well in this new environment. I was so blessed to have a son as socially skilled as Tyler was (and very much still is).

There were two ladies that I will never forget; they were so helpful and courteous and loving toward both of us. Martha saw me standing behind a post and came up to me and asked me to sit with her while they were finishing up their program. I could not look this woman in the eye at all. Something within me told me that if I did not make eye contact, I would be okay. But I knew once I made that connection, I might "lose it."

Martha and Debbie have been instrumental in how Tyler has overcome all of these obstacles. In fact, they were special to me as well, because they would extend themselves to comfort me. On Valentine's Day that year, Martha left a vase of flowers at my front doorstep so I would see them when I arrived home.

God has brought so many people into our lives. As two people without any family, over time we began to realize how much family we truly had. Family should not to be measured by a blood connection, but by the heart.

The Sunday after Stan's death, Tyler insisted that we visit the church. Martha picked him up and took him to Sunday school. It would have been so easy to stay at home, but I had promised Tyler that I would go to the church service. I don't remember getting there, and I don't remember getting home. I don't remember what the sermon was. I don't remember what songs were sung. I don't remember if I cried or not. I was not in this world; I was in my own, trying not to be visible in this world at all. What I do remember is something that always puts a smile on my face, something I try to recall when I feel frightened and alone. What I remember is sitting in a pew that Sunday and feeling completely alone as I looked at young couples together, and I remember telling God how angry I was because Stan had wanted to be here with me—that had been our plan.

I looked up into the faces of the choir members—searching for something. I did not know what I was looking for, but I recognized it when I found it. Out of all those faces, one stood out among the rest. There was a woman who sang with joy. She lifted her voice in praise, and it showed all over her face. She smiled and swayed, and you could just tell she was something special. She sang with joy in her heart.

That face was what I looked for each Sunday after that. I did not know who she was, but her face and her smile brought the only time of peace I had that week. It eased my heart. You could say that her smile was what gave me the strength to go to church each Sunday. Isn't God amazing in how he can use the most unlikely people to help others overcome extraordinary circumstances and obstacles?

After a couple of weeks, people from the church were really beginning to show their generosity, and we began to experience the truth of what it means to be part of a church family. There was a very beautiful snowfall. It was the first real snow for Tyler (and Rocky) to see and play in.

I received a call from a gentleman at the church who had met Tyler at the un-birthday party, and he wanted to come by and bring some lasagna. (How did they know this was Tyler's favorite food?) Doug came by and brought an entire meal—and a sled for Tyler to play in the snow. I could not look Doug in the eye because I felt like a charity case. All those times I had helped others throughout the years—had I made them feel like charity cases? This taught me so much about how I reach out to others in the things I say and do. One of the things that Doug told me as we stood in my kitchen—I was uncomfortable with letting a man into any part of the house—Doug told me that if I did not accept what he and his family were bringing to us, then they would be unable to fulfill what God had called upon them to do. That has stuck with me, and I share that with many other widows when they find it difficult to be gracious receivers.

Three weeks after Stan's death, Tyler decided he wanted to join the church. I sat with our neighbors and was scared to death. I was not sure this was something I wanted to do. It was not right to do this without Stan; nothing was right without having Stan there with me. Charlotte asked if I would like her to go up to the front with us, and I had tears coming down my face. I told her no. I needed to learn to do some things on my own. At invitation time, Tyler and I walked down the aisle to the front of the church and completed the paperwork. Tyler had accepted Christ and wanted to be baptized.

As we were introduced to the church, we remained standing until the service was over. Then we were greeted by members of the church. I looked over, and, as I looked up, there was a woman in her choir robe coming down to greet me with the biggest smile I had ever seen! I couldn't believe that this woman, who had no idea how much peace she brought into my life each Sunday morning, was going to take the time to meet with me and introduce herself. I cannot tell you what it meant to me. She introduced herself, and I honestly did not remember her name until later (her name was Sherrie). What a sweet woman of God this lady has been in my life. Again, God sent me a "sister": a friend who would turn out to be a very valuable part of my spiritual growth.

I do not recall everything that happened during those first few weeks. I don't remember the people whose paths crossed mine or things that were said. I was so caught up in being the best I could for Tyler. But it wasn't easy, because no one knew me on a personal level: they only knew us for the circumstances we were going through.

I found a remarkable Sunday school class of women from all walks of life and ages. I was the baby and loved it! This class was made up of career women, caretakers, homemakers, widows, divorced women, and those who had never married. The one thing they all had in common was their love for our Lord Jesus Christ. I was placed into their lives for a reason: to be nurtured, loved, and prayed over. With these ladies, I never had to explain a thing; I was immediately accepted and loved. God placed me in this class. After a couple of visits, I found out that Sherrie (Ms. Smiley) was a member.

I was placed in this particular church, Sunday school class, and neighborhood not only to receive love and kindness, but to allow others to follow their hearts and extend themselves in remarkable and blessed ways. I wish I could sit down and explain every person in full detail, but they all know who they are and what they did. For that I will be forever grateful.

One of the most difficult things for me was to tell people when I had a need. I wouldn't let anyone in the back of the house because they might find out that I didn't have a bed. I was still sleeping on those cots. One of the first things Stan and I were supposed to do when I arrived was to buy a regular bed. We had always had a waterbed, but we had decided to not bring it with us. I do not recall how the subject came up, but Charlotte and Randy had an extra box spring, mattress, and frame. At some point, they brought it over to the house so I could begin sleeping in a bed. God was in such control!

I received a check for two hundred fifty dollars from a lady that I did not know. Her sweet note said it was from their Sunday school class; they had felt that they should send Tyler and me some money. I was caught off guard by the generosity of so many that did not know me at all. I held onto that check (after writing a thank-you note), and would not use it for groceries or anything that I needed—until the washing machine went out.

I would not call Randy or anyone else to help me, so I moved the washer (filled with water) from upstairs to the driveway. I thought I was going to kill myself doing this; pride had stepped into action. These were all things that Stan was supposed to handle. I shopped around until I found the cheapest washing machine I could find, and guess what? The check the Sunday school class had sent me was just enough to cover it! That tells you how cheap it was, but it really shows how generous God is in how he uses others.

Not long after that, the dryer went out, and I just broke down into tears. Charlotte walked over in the middle of my crisis. Together we were able to solve that as well, but Randy insisted on picking it up for me. Someone was getting rid of their dryer, and they donated it to the cause! Again, God was in control.

I wrote the woman who had sent me the two hundred fifty dollars; her name was Julia. Julia became a very close friend. After talking on the phone a few times and finding out that I walked almost every day, she decided she would join me. In my mind, I could imagine what this woman looked like. She had to be six feet tall and slinky because her voice was so sweet and caring and she was just so special. She drove up in a big car, and, when she got out, I stopped walking and tried to figure out where the rest of her had gone. Julia was barely five feet tall, but she had a heart that is bigger than Dallas.

I was so blessed, and I did not even know it. I was so caught up in the things that had gone wrong in my life and feeling sorry for myself that I couldn't see that God was ever-present in even the smallest of things.

A few weeks after joining my Sunday school class of godly women, I felt a push to visit a singles class. I don't know why—because I did not feel single. In my heart, I was still married. One Sunday, I had every intention of going, but I panicked and ran home. (I left my car at the church and ran home!) The next Sunday, it was as though something was pushing me to go into that room...which I did accomplish. It was the last time I would ever walk into that singles class. I am sure I would have felt the same way regardless of where it was, because I did not believe I was single and it was just too soon.

I walked into the singles class, and immediately the women stared and glared as if I was the new competition. They were not friendly; in fact, they were stand-offish. The men in that room...how can I possibly explain this? The men smiled and stared at me like they were thinking, "Hmm, fresh meat!"

I found my way to a chair and just sat there. It was nothing like being with my ladies. With them, as soon as I walked in the door, I was greeted with a hug, a smile, and sweetness. A woman (whose name I do not recall) gave me two magazines, which I quickly placed in my Bible. I never made eye contact with anyone. All I remember is looking at the floor and inspecting shoes. I was doing all I could to disassociate myself completely. The woman asked me to tell my story. I could not believe it. I did not have a story, much less one that I was willing to share! But I stated that my husband had died a few weeks earlier, and I do not recall anything else that was said. The class continued, and I sat there trying to figure out why in the world I was there! They did not even pray together!

Sherrie called me that afternoon and prayed with me and talked to me. I told her that I could not figure out why I was supposed to be in that Sunday school class. Because I lived in her neighborhood—isn't God good in how he strategically plans things?—Sherrie would sometimes stop by and check up on me, and pray with me, just to be there. Later that evening, I opened my Bible to do my devotional, and I had completely forgotten about the magazines that the woman from the singles class had given me. Both of them were called *Christian Single*. I looked through one of them, and then I opened the second one. The page I had turned to featured an article called "Suddenly Single." I read the article and could not believe what I was reading. It was an article about young widows and widowers, and everything it stated was exactly what I was going through.

I called Sherrie and told her about what I had discovered. I did not realize at the time what I was being called to do. I was being called to start a widows' ministry to minister to the hearts and spiritual growth of the ladies. This is something that was missing in the churches. I did not know then how true that was—and that later I would become the founder of Widow2Widow™, a 501(c)(3) non-profit organization.

At the time of this writing, it has been five years since Stan's death, and my life is very different now. Back then, at the age of thirty-seven, I felt my future had been taken away from me. I felt as if I had been robbed or violated somehow. It has taken me a long time to stop asking God the question, "Why? Why did Stan have to die?" Instead, I ask God what I am to learn from all of this and how he wants to use me. This did not happen overnight, and I still struggle with it at times.

I wish my mother and grandmother were alive today to see how far I have come because of God's grace and unconditional love. When Stan died, Mother and Grandma were alive, but Mother had a mental illness and was in a nursing home in Nevada; Grandma was in Texas suffering from Alzheimer's. I was completely alone, at least until I was blessed with that ladies' Sunday school class—filled with sisters with whom I had never shared and other mothers.

Grandma was one unique woman. When asked to describe her, I usually say, "You see me—you have met my grandmother." She had a heart filled with compassion for others. Now, that is not to say that you wanted to speak politics with her. If you wanted to get into a curse-filled debate with her...you would have been warned!

Grandma was a fine Southern Christian woman. She widowed in her late forties. My grandfather died when I was an infant. Grandma definitely had her opinions, and she would let you know about them. You knew where you stood with her at all times. I am pretty much the same way, but softer. (My son, however, might dispute the "softer" part.)

However, Grandma was an alcoholic. When I was very young, she went through a period of time when I saw her crying a lot. It was when she was drinking. I think that is one reason that Mother got hooked on prescription drugs: it was a hereditary addiction and one that I have refused to let consume my life. I will not even take Tylenol unless it is absolutely necessary.

There were many similarities between Mother and Grandma, but the difference was that Grandma overcame her addictions through her faith. Mother continued with hers until it ultimately destroyed her.

The only time I went to church, as a young child, was when I was visiting Grandma. Yet, because of her addiction and other things, I grew confused as I got older. But when I went off to college, I lived within seventy miles of her. We became so close that if your grandmother could be your soul mate, she was mine. Grandma was there when I was baptized, and it was so wonderful to see her reaction and to have her there to share it with me. Grandma was the first person I told about my engagement to Stan, and the first person I told when I became pregnant with Tyler.

In February 2004, I had the honor to speak at a new widows' group that had formed in Tyler, Texas. Because I was finally home (the second time since Stan's death), I drove to Athens, Texas, to visit my grandmother. I knew that she would not know who I was, but I felt that I needed to go and see her. I never could stand the smell of nursing homes; some are better than others, but the smell in this one was so bad that it just took your breath away.

I got to Grandma's room, and she was sitting up, asleep. I sat there and looked around her room, and I could not imagine that after having a fulfilled life, this was all that was left. I stayed there for over an hour and held her hand, caressed her face, and talked to her.

I recalled the last time we were together before she completely lost all of her faculties. I had sat her up on the bed and held her hand and shared; I knew it would probably not be much longer before she would not remember who I was. I continued to tell her how much I loved her, and what her presence in my life had meant. I did not know, at the time, how true that would be. I touch the lives of others with what God has placed in my heart just as my grandmother's life touched others because of her faith and willingness to help those who needed to be comforted.

Grandma awoke, and I began to sing her favorite hymn, "The Old Rugged Cross." She looked over, as if she knew who I was, and she began to mumble. As I continued to sing to her and talk to her, a look came over her that made me think that she perhaps recognized me for just a split second. She did this several times. I asked her if it was okay to give her a hug, and she put her face out so it would touch mine. A tear rolled down her face. I told her how much I loved her and had missed her, and I told her about all the work I was doing that God had called me to do. I held her face and looked into her eyes and I told her it was okay to let go and to move on; we would all be okay.

Three weeks later, I got the call that Grandma had passed away. When she had, a preacher and some ladies had come by and were singing hymns. Grandma had looked up with a smile on her face and reached out with her arms, and then she was gone—to be with the Lord and to be reunited with all of her loved ones who had gone home before her.

I was blessed to have such a fine and strong grandmother to show me so many things. It was her strength and her faith, I realized, that had gotten me through many difficult times in my life, such as the journey into and through widowhood.

3

The First Holidays

The holidays had always been such a fun time in our family. We would all gather at Grandma's house, with presents covering half of her living room, because we had grown into such a large family. So when it came time to face the holidays alone for the first time in my life, I succumbed to a great deal of depression.

On the first Thanksgiving following Stan's death, I sent Tyler to be with our friends, the Dunns. They were leaving Thanksgiving morning for east Tennessee and would return on Friday. I didn't want Tyler to miss out on the holidays when it was something that I just could not do. I dropped him off at their house and had every intention of going home and feeling sorry for myself.

As I was driving home, I got a call from my young Hispanic widow friend who had lost her husband that May to a car accident. Letty was about thirty-two or so at the time and had a three-year-old son named Austin.

Letty wanted me to come over to her in-laws and talk with her for a while. She was struggling so hard to get through the same things I was experiencing. After her continued persistence, I agreed and drove over to their house to visit. I intended to stay only for a little while so I could get home and cry without Tyler there.

But God had other plans because, by the time the day was over, we had covered so many things. I shared in a hurting family's holiday. The Sunday after Thanksgiving, they all joined my church, and Letty accepted Christ as her savior. Letty, being Hispanic, had been raised Catholic, but her husband was Baptist and had visited our church a couple of times before his death. Letty had so many questions about our faith. I have been so blessed since our meeting together; we became more than just nominal friends. I got her involved in our Sunday school class and watched her grow.

Our first Christmas without Stan is one that I will never forget, and one that to this day gives me compassion for widows and others who are hurting. Tyler and I did not decorate that Christmas because I had every intention of us going back to Texas for the holiday. But as the time drew nearer, I just could not make myself go. Being around others without Stan was more than I could handle. I suffered one panic attack after another during that time.

I did not share our plans with others—or, actually, at this point, our lack of them. As far as everyone was concerned, we were going to Texas. I did not want them to feel they had to include us in their plans. I would have felt like an intruder, and I was already dealing with enough loneliness as it was.

At the time, our church held services on Friday night. Tyler and I went, in order to avoid being at home. What I had not expected was for someone to ask why we had not gone to Texas, as planned.

Tyler was in youth choir, and he loved his leaders, Tom and Peggy. Peggy was singing in the service that evening. Tyler ran up to her (as I sat quietly in the back), and the next thing I knew, he was running up to me, telling me that Ms. Peggy wanted to talk to me. I walked over to her, and evidently she had asked Tyler why we had not gone to Texas. His explanation had been that Mom just couldn't do it.

Peggy asked what our plans for Christmas Day were, and I told her we would be spending the day together, just the two of us. She looked up at me, smiled (a smile that I would learn to love over the years), and asked Tyler and me to join her and her family for Christmas dinner. I could not look her in the eye. I looked over at Tyler, and he was excited about getting to go over there and have a Christmas with Ms. Peggy and Mr. Tom. I said no (again, not looking her in the eye), but I looked over at Tyler again, and something within me said yes, we would go.

I did not know this woman very well. All I knew was that she led the youth choir, she sang in the church choir, and she had a beautiful voice that I since have called upon many times to sing.

Sunday was Christmas Eve, and I was not going to miss out on my Sunday school class that morning. Those ladies were such a blessing, just as they always were. After Sunday school, I went to the church service and noticed that Peggy was singing in the service that morning. I was so excited to hear her voice again. She was really something to watch when she sang. God blessed her tremendously with the gift of her voice and her ability to deliver it. Every time I heard Peggy sing and watched her, I was just in awe of the talent she possessed, and it gave me such joy and peace.

Peggy came up to me and said she needed to come by the house that afternoon to bring something. I told her that if she had it with her, she should just give it to me. (We lived in an apartment townhouse, not a real house.) She said that she would need to bring it because it would not fit in my car. I could not imagine what it could possibly be, but I did not give it much thought until that afternoon.

Later that afternoon, Peggy called and asked for directions. She drove up in a silver Lexus SUV. I was beginning to think, why in the world would this woman want to take time out to bring me something? When Stan was alive, I'd never had thoughts of feeling unworthy; why was I having such a difficult time now that I was a widow?

Tyler and I met her outside. She opened the back of her SUV and began to pull out a partially decorated Christmas tree with lights. I will never forget the look on Tyler's face as she helped him carry it into the house. His eyes were so big, and he was excited for the first time in a long time. I looked over at her. Not one word was spoken, but we both had tears in our eyes and rolling down our cheeks.

We got the tree set up, and Peggy brought in even more decorations so Tyler could decorate the tree. He plugged in the tree, and his face beamed as brightly as the lights on the tree.

Peggy went back outside to her car and returned with big sacks of presents for Tyler and me. I looked over at her as she wiped a tear from her face. She made the comment that she did not understand what was happening to her, because she never did anything like this. But when she saw the look on Tyler's face, she knew why she was supposed to do this: God told her to, and she was being obedient to the call.

I wanted to understand as well, but I felt like a charity case—not because of Peggy's graciousness, but because we had always been the givers. Being a gracious receiver was not something I was very good at.

We had already received Christmas presents from the singles department at the church, so we were able to put presents under the tree and wait for Christmas morning. Of course, Tyler reminded me of our tradition of opening one present on Christmas Eve.

Christmas morning came, and honestly, I was not prepared for how I would feel. For months, I would not allow myself to truly cry…but on Christmas, I cried and cried and cried some more, thinking about how fun the holidays used to be when we were together as a family. I thought about our last Christmas together and how we were approaching the one-year mark since Stan's death. I could not believe the pain I was feeling on this Christmas Day. I cried so much that my eyes became swollen.

Soon it was time to get ready and head over to Tom and Peggy's home. I did not want to go and share in someone else's Christmas. I just couldn't—but Tyler was so looking forward to it. We drove over there, and I had every intention of dropping him off, going home, and crawling back into bed to wish the day away. But God knew what I would do, and he made sure I was greeted as soon as we drove up to the huge, beautiful home in which I knew I would not feel comfortable at all.

As we walked in, we were welcomed by all of Peggy's family, including Tom's mother, who had become a widow the previous May. We just talked and talked, and I felt very welcome in their home. We ended up staying until late in the evening, and a friendship formed like no other I had ever shared.

This friendship began because of a tree. Peggy and I would need one another in the weeks, months, and years ahead.

4

Life Seems to Be Filled with Sorrow

January 2001 was a time for change in my life. I tried very hard to overcome my fear of January. January 8 marked nine years since Daddy had passed away. January 10 marked one year since Stan's death—the day our whole world changed. But I had this feeling about something that I could not explain.

I talked to my mother on January 8 and 10. We talked and talked, like we had never spoken before. She sounded so excited when I called her. Mother had been in a nursing home in Nevada, under some very strenuous circumstances. On one hand I wanted her near me, but our relationship had always been better when there was distance between us. My uncle called me that week because he knew how tough it was going to be for me. We discussed Mother and her health. I told Uncle Jim that I had a feeling something was going to happen, and, if Mother survived the week from January 8 to January 14, then perhaps the feeling was about something else.

I called Mother again on January 12, and at first she sounded so sad until she heard my voice and knew it was me. She began to tell me how proud of me she was. (This was something Mother had never said to me before.) I told her I would call her when I got home after church on Sunday. She proceeded to caution me about my telephone bill, and I laughed and told her I needed to hear her voice to help me get through.

I got up that Sunday morning full of energy and hope for the first time in ages. That morning, I told my Sunday school class about how I had gotten through my first year and how excited I was about what God had planned, since I would hold our first widows' meeting in February.

When Tyler and I got home from church, there were a couple of calls on my answering machine. Using the caller ID, I recognized the area code of one, and figured it was from the nursing home in Nevada. I figured Mother had wanted to beat me to the phone this time.

There was a message on the machine from the director of the nursing home, asking me to call them as soon as I got the message. I called, and they proceeded to tell me that Mother had died around 7:00 AM (our time), in her sleep. I couldn't believe it: the feeling I was afraid of had proven prescient. It was January 14.

All my life I had been able to sense things, and I felt as if I was cursed sometimes, but I only feel it when I am close to someone. It isn't just the bad things, yet I seem to be more sensitive when it is.

The phone rang again, and it was my uncle. He confirmed what I had already heard.

On one hand, I was upset. Here I was, having to deal with yet another loss; on the other hand, I was relieved because I was never going to have to walk on eggshells again to know how Mother would react to even the smallest of things.

Mother was diagnosed late in life as being massively bipolar and schizophrenic, and she was hooked on prescription drugs, so she was not the easiest person to live with. When Mother wanted to be nice, you couldn't ask for a better person to be around. Unfortunately, she was not that way very often. She was abusive to Daddy, and she was abusive to my brother and me.

My earliest memory of her was when I was about three years old. She had sat my brother Pat and me on her bed. She had pulled a chair up, then put a gun to her head, and said that we had driven her to do that. She would go into rages, and Pat, who was six years older than me, would scoop me up and lock me in a closet, telling me to be quiet. I assumed he ran out of the house until her rage was over. He would come back, get me out of the closet, and then take a beating for defying her.

Pat had run away several times. But as soon as he could, he joined the Army and left me. I was beaten; I was told that I was not worthy of her love, that I was never going to be pretty, and that I would never amount to anything. I watched how she treated Daddy and how hurt he always was.

Daddy traveled all the time, but I do not know how much he wanted to learn about what was happening when he was not there. Daddy and I were very close, and I think Mother resented that because I was not the daughter she had wanted. I liked to hunt, and to fish, and to be with Daddy—because it took me away from her.

Mother had been married three times before she was twenty-one. Daddy was her last husband. Pat is actually my half-brother. Mother was pregnant with him when she and Daddy married, but he was not Daddy's biological son. However, Daddy always raised him as such, and we did not know the truth until we were grown.

All of this made our lives unbearable at times. Mother was finally diagnosed with her mental illnesses, and then Pat left her alone in Nevada. It was time to make some decisions the summer after Stan died (which was the summer before Mother died). I forgave her for everything and told her so. Those last few months with my Mother were worth an entire lifetime of the unhappiness.

I know God placed it on my heart to forgive her, and I praise him for that. If there is someone you need to forgive, do so. If they die before you have the chance, you will spend the remainder of your life regretting your decision, and then Satan will have won.

I have forgiven my brother for everything, but I have not been able to locate him to tell him. We have not spoken or seen each other since Daddy's funeral in January 1992. I pray every day for a reunion, or at least an opportunity to send him a letter telling him how I feel. But I do not know how much of the mental illness he has—or if he is in any condition to understand.

As the afternoon of January 14 progressed, all I needed to do became more real to me. I made a few phone calls, one of them to the caregivers of my mother. I gave instructions to have my mother cremated and said that I would make arrangements to come to Nevada to pick up her things.

It was during this time that I began to go into a deep depression because everyone I loved had either died or was no longer mentally capable of being there when I needed them the most. By thirty-eight years of age, I had buried a child, my father, my husband, and now my mother. All I had left was Tyler, or so I thought.

Over time, I began to love and be loved by my new mothers, grandmothers, and even sisters as Widow2Widow™ had begun to form. I could take my pain and use it to help others in ways I had never imagined.

I was unsure how I was going to manage the finances to get to Nevada and take care of Mother's things. But God had a plan. He used Tommye, a new widow who had often called me her daughter of the heart, since she had two natural daughters already. Tommye knew my situation and paid for my plane ticket to Salt Lake City, Utah, where I would rent an SUV (it was January and I needed to go up into the mountains of Nevada) and take care of Mother's final arrangements.

Because I was having Mother cremated (as per her wishes), I waited a week before I flew out there. God had planned all of the necessities, like who would take care of Tyler while I was there. My dear friends Tom and Peggy offered to take care of him for me.

I was only going to be gone two nights. I arrived in Salt Lake City and had a few hours' drive ahead of me. I was nervous because the last time I had made the trip to see Mother, it was with Stan and Tyler. Because I had never gone alone, I was unsure how to handle the roads if there was snow.

But, of course, God protected me in every way on the trip. I arrived in Ely, Nevada, and checked into the hotel that was near the nursing home where my mother had lived for three years. The last time (and only time) I had been there was Thanksgiving, 1999.

We had just found out in July 1999 where she had been taken. Mother had been living in Texas and had gotten so bad that my uncle had called my brother, telling him to come get her. Pat took Mother up there, immediately put her in the facility, and took all of her belongings. He had never came back to see her. Mother became a ward of the State of Nevada before I was even told where she was.

For over a year, Mother did not have any visitors until Stan, Tyler, and I traveled to be with her on that Thanksgiving. I knew, looking at the condition she was in, that it would be the last time I would ever see my mother alive.

After I got checked into the hotel, I drove over to the nursing home and was hit with the smell that I hate in those places. I knew I wasn't feeling well, but I also knew I had a job to do. The nurses took me to Mother's room, and I had expected that they would have gone through everything as I had instructed, but they had left the room exactly the way Mother had died in it. She had a private room, and it overlooked the mountains of Nevada. It was beautiful to look out of her huge window. I sat on the side of Mother's bed, not believing the nurses had not touched anything of hers. Even the bed had not been made. I don't know if the sheets were the same sheets that Mother died in or not, but I lay there and held the sheets up to my face, trying to smell her, to feel her—anything at all.

Though our relationship had been rocky for many years, I missed her. I sat there remembering the last time we had visited and how we had taken her shopping and out to eat. Mother was barely five feet tall and only weighed seventy-eight pounds. We were like "Mutt and Jeff," because I was tall and overweight. In fact, when I arrived at the nursing home, I told the nurses who I was, and they asked where my sister was. I told them I didn't have a sister. I had lost over a hundred pounds since they had seen me last, and they couldn't believe it was me. Mother would have been so proud to see the weight off. It was one of the things she had always disliked about Daddy and me: our weight.

I began to go through Mother's things. She had kept every letter I had sent her while she was there. She had even started a letter to me that was dated January 12, after we'd had our conversation about her being proud of me. The letter was not finished, but it is something I cherish. As I was going through her clothes and belongings, I got hot and clammy and had to run to be outside in the cold, crisp air. I don't know if I was coming down with something, if it was a panic attack, or if I was just distraught and overwhelmed because of losing my mother. It could have been simply the high altitude.

I went back to her room, stacked up the clothes, took what I felt I would want later on, and left the other things behind. I talked with the staff of the nursing home about giving away what was left. (I certainly didn't need her clothes.) I had sent her some packages for Christmas. I had sent one package every other day for three weeks with instructions to open one package every other day. I really hadn't been able to afford it, but I had wanted her to have something to look forward to at the holidays; after all, she had not received any visitors since we were there in November 1999.

There were many boxes left unopened. I had sent her clothes. She loved orange slices, and she had some of those. Mother loved to have perfectly manicured nails, and I had sent her supplies for that, as well as makeup and hair stuff. There were notepads and stamps. She had things like that, which were unopened. I donated all of it to the nursing home, to be distributed among the residents.

I loaded up my rental car with items. I would repack them in my suitcase to take back home with me. I drove around Ely for a little while before heading to my room to rest, just remembering being there the last time. Not too long after I arrived, my uncle called to check up on me and to make sure everything had gone okay. I had an appointment the next morning at the funeral home to get Mother's ashes and the jewelry she had been wearing. He was concerned about me. I reassured him that I was hanging in there, but inside I was just numb. My head was hurting, but it was because of the high altitude there; I was not accustomed to it.

The next morning, as I was checking out of the hotel, Gayle from my church called my cell phone. I remember loading my car while I was on the phone with her. As I got into the vehicle, listening to her sweet, soft, and reassuring voice, I looked up, and there was the mountain where we had taken Mother on Thanksgiving Day in 1999. It was covered in snow, but the early-morning sun was shining brightly on the mountain. It was glistening with beauty. Its backdrop was the clearest, deepest blue sky I had ever seen. Gayle prayed with me over the phone because she knew that I was not going to be bringing Mother's ashes with me to

Tennessee. I was traveling to the top of that mountain to release them in memory of Mother.

I found the funeral home. It was an old historic home that had been renovated to work as a funeral home. I signed the papers, and they gave me Mother's jewelry in a little bag. It was very impersonal, but they didn't know her, or me, for that matter.

I took the box that contained her ashes and clung to them all the way out to the car. I had to take a deep breath because I could feel a panic attack coming on. I sat there in prayer, holding onto the heavy little box and thinking, how can someone die like this, alone? After living on earth for sixty-plus years, this was all there was left of her.

A snowstorm was expected to come through later in the day, although at the moment, the sky didn't show any signs of a winter storm. I needed to get up that mountain and do what I had come to do. I found the road, and it was as desolate as I remembered. It was obvious that no one had traveled up this mountain since the last snowstorm, and I knew that there was one spot that could be very treacherous if I was not careful. I put the SUV into four-wheel drive and slowly began to creep up the mountain.

Somehow it was more gorgeous than I remembered. This time, there was snow everywhere you could see. I continued up the mountain. It was taking a long time, since I was not accustomed to driving in the snow. I reached the point where I had prayed to be careful because if something happened, no one would know: that is how desolate it truly was.

I reached that particular point, and God had answered the prayer, because it was the only place where the snow had melted as the sun shone on it. I could not stop, because I was afraid I wouldn't be able to get going again, but I just praised God for being in that vehicle with me—on this outing that was harder than I had ever thought it would be.

I reached the top of the mountain, and it was clear and quiet. There was such a calm and cold crispness in the air. I got out of the SUV and stepped into snow that came up to about an inch below my knee. I smiled. I could not explain the peace that had suddenly suffused my body.

I treaded over to the benches where we had all sat together just a little over a year before. I cleared off about a foot of snow from the table and just sat there. I looked over to the valley and at other mountains and just listened to the quiet of the place where I was about to say good-bye. Without realizing it, I was not only saying good-bye to Mother, but I was also going to be finalizing my good-bye to Stan.

I sat on that table for what seemed to be an eternity. I saw deer tracks and some other small animal tracks that had been made since the last snow, and I remembered all of the good times I had shared with my mother. I never allowed myself to think about the bad times. I stood up and opened the box of ashes, and I put my hand in there and felt around them. It was hard to comprehend that this was all there was of her and her existence on earth. I scattered her ashes and began to cry as I told her good-bye, because I was also telling Stan good-bye. It was something that I had not truly done with him. Both times, I had been basically alone. How fitting it was to be there at that moment, giving honor and glory to God for their lives, because it was the roles they had played—both in life and in death—that had caused me to be on the path that I was on. It was a path directed by God, and I was truly blessed on top of that mountain, finding peace.

I drove down the mountain in the same tracks I had made coming up, and it dawned on me that I was freezing. I had not been prepared for the cold weather and walking around in the snow. Praise God for the invention of good heaters in vehicles.

When I got down to the bottom of the mountain, I called Peggy and checked to see how Tyler had been doing. She talked to me for the longest time. I don't recall everything we spoke about, but it was her voice and her love for us that helped me avoid breaking down, as all of the emotions of having to say goodbye to my Mother, and not having Stan with me and the realization of how alone I truly was going to feel as I drove back to Salt Lake City.

Several hours later that evening, I found my hotel, and once again my uncle called to check on me. I explained to him in detail what it was like as I had released Mother and said good-bye. I was to catch the plane the next morning for home, and I was actually looking forward to the next phase in my life and what God had to offer.

5

Life Goes On

February 2001 marked the first official meeting of the Widow2Widow™ ministry. We were not sure what to expect, but Peggy agreed to sing a couple of songs for us and to share what turned out to be the first of many things to come.

Gayle was present to offer all of the inspiration that was needed and also to share in this first for our church—and for any church at that time. Rosann was my Sunday school teacher at the time, and she had agreed to be our first guest speaker. She was to speak on the topic of self-esteem. Somehow, as widows on this new journey, we lose our self-esteem in some sense—as well as losing our identities.

We had almost forty ladies attending this meeting. Some were only there to see what it was all about; some were not quite ready to face the idea that the word *widow* actually applied to them. But most were there because God had sent them, and they knew this was something they needed in their lives to help them mature on this walk and to know they were not alone.

We shared in a lot of laughter that day. I had asked Tommye, the first widow to whom I had ministered, to give her testimony of what the ministry already meant in her life. I told the ladies that I was young enough to be their daughter or granddaughter, and yet I had walked on the journey, and I was still walking on the journey. I told them that they had something to learn from each person there, even me.

This was to be the first meeting of many for Brentwood Baptist Church, and a ministry was born that would grow to span several states and to touch the hearts of many widows. I knew that the calling that was made upon my life was to hold the burden of anyone out there who was hurting, particularly widows, because churches and families are commanded to care for the widows in James 1:27.

I honestly believe that if churches knew about the ministry, they would adopt it. But the downside has been in trying to educate churches that the needs of widows actually do exist within their own congregations. The stereotype of widows is that we are all older and that we are all left wealthy. I did not fit into either of those profiles, and we had moved here to a community where we had not known anyone. But what I have learned is that God is faithful. I don't know why—and I may never know—but my faith in God and his promises for me will not fail.

This ministry opened a whole new world for me. I gained confidence in the abilities that God had given to me. I found myself feeling worthy again because I was able to take my circumstances and turn them around to help hundreds, perhaps even thousands, of other women.

We all have purpose in life. The problem is that when a tragedy strikes, we want to curl up in a shell. Most of us never step outside that comfort zone and truly grieve—and then learn how to experience joy again, to embrace life.

That is what the ministry is all about: to help the ladies know they are not alone and to help them find purpose in their lives. God calls widows to prayer. That is an honor, and yet the churches do not understand this. If they did, they would place the widows up high enough to govern the prayers within the church bodies.

One morning, I looked into the mirror and began to cry. Tyler came in and asked if I was having another "moment." Whenever I cried, he called it a "moment." I told him that yes, I was having a "moment," but I was almost forty years old and could have "moments" for things other than just missing his daddy. Tyler asked me why was I crying, and I told him to look at my eyes. I asked him where the wrinkles had come from. Tyler laughed and said they were not wrinkles: they were dimples at my eyes. I just hugged that boy, thinking he was the most wonderful preteen male on this earth—until he opened his mouth again. He said, "Besides, Mom, you just lost a whole lot of weight; where do you think they have been hiding?" I rushed him out of the room, telling him never to return. I have learned to laugh about it now—it is cute, isn't it?

In all of this, I have learned to live again. I have learned to laugh again. I actually did not have to learn to laugh again, but had to give myself permission to laugh. But at the same time, I had to let my heart love again.

The spring of 2001 began a year of remarkable changes. Widow2Widow™ had formed. I had lost my mother and had begun to come to terms with her death and Stan's. Tyler was still struggling and making bad decisions. Both of us were depressed, but major changes were happening for both of us that would change the course of our lives.

It was during this time that Peggy had me go to her gynecologist because in conversation, I had told her I had not been for a checkup since moving to Tennessee and that I was terrified of gynecologists! I was having panic attacks on a regular basis, not sleeping very much, and forgetting to eat. She told me that I was depressed, and that these were signs she had recognized in herself before.

So I went to her doctor, and what a sweet man he was. Peggy had to have called him, though, and warned him about my fear, because no sooner had I signed in and completed the paperwork than they took me back! My blood pressure was through the roof, which it always is when I go to one of them. They took me back to meet Dr. P., and the first thing he did was make me feel at ease. He introduced himself and prayed with me. He took me to the examination room and said he would be right back. I barely had enough time to get undressed before he came back in. He did his thing and was out of there.

I got dressed and was escorted back to his office, where he was waiting. He shut the door and proceeded to ask me about my life. I broke down and cried. He ended up putting me on an antidepressant, and, when I asked him how long I needed to be on them, he asked how old Tyler was. He said that I would need to be on them until Tyler was at least seventeen years old. I cried and cried, and he just held my hand and told me it would be okay. It was during this time that I shared with him the problems I was having with Tyler, and how he was doing things that were so out of character for him.

That afternoon, I took Tyler to see his new general practitioner. The doctor checked him over and talked to each of us separately. I told him all about what Tyler was doing and said that I thought he, too, might be suffering from depression (after all, it runs in my family). The doctor prescribed something for Tyler as well, and, when I asked him how long Tyler needed to be on it, he said maybe six months—if that long. So I began to cry all over again. Something just didn't seem right about me having to stay on them until he was seventeen, when he only needed to take them for six months! Needless to say, I did not have to stay on them!

Tyler was still playing baseball, a sport his dad had loved. In the spring of 2001, I signed him up again, and he ended up playing on a team with some people that he knew from church. In March or April, a friend introduced her brother-in-law, Larry, to me. He had come out to watch his nephew David play baseball. Larry just stood there, and he did not seem to be a very happy man. We met again in early May and again in the latter part of that month. Each time Larry became more talkative, but he still seemed to be very unhappy: he never smiled. He was intimidating, actually, because he was very tall, six-foot-four or more, and he had a gotee on his face that made him appear older than he was.

I did not really give him much thought until June. Tyler and I were on our first vacation by ourselves in Florida, and, as I was on the beach, Larry's name came to mind. It shocked me because I could not imagine why in the world this would happen.

We returned home from our vacation, and I had a message from Larry, who had called that very day I had been on the beach. He explained how he had gotten my number and asked me to call him back.

I did not have a chance to decide if I would call him back or not because he ended up calling me again. He said that he usually called three times, and, if there was no response, that was it. Larry asked both Tyler and me out for a date. I was scared to death. The only thing I knew was that he had a Christian family. I talked to Tyler and told him about the conversation, and Tyler's first reaction was, "What if he is psychotic?" I told him the thought had crossed my mind. But we knew his family, and, after all, Larry had asked us both out on a date.

So we agreed to go out with this man. It was awkward because I had not been on a date since Stan and I had dated. On that first date, Larry took us out for dinner and then to play miniature golf. We talked and talked and talked. He had not been aware that I was a young widow. He had made the assumption, as many others do, that because I was a young mother, I must be divorced. Larry asked me how I managed to appear happy, with all that I had been through. I told him it was because of my relationship with Jesus Christ and that I had learned the difference between joy and happiness. Joy is a gift from God and should be shared even in the darkest moments of life. Happiness is based on circumstances.

It had been thirty years since Larry had been in church, but he began to go with Tyler and me because he knew how important it was us. Unless he was working on any particular Sunday, he was there with us.

We dated for six weeks and talked constantly. Larry told me about his marriage that had ended in divorce. He had then fallen in love with JoAnn, the love of his life. JoAnn had died of cancer before they were to be married. Larry had never really gotten over the pain of losing her, and, over the years, he had become more and more depressed. In October 2000, he had bought a Harley-Davidson because he had decided he would end his pain by committing suicide. He had the spot picked out, and he was going to commit suicide in June 2001—the month God had made our paths cross and we had begun dating.

After six weeks of dating, Larry asked Tyler for his permission to marry me. Tyler could hardly wait. He cared for Larry so much, and he asked if, once we were married, he could call Larry "Dad." Tyler was thirteen then, and with an open heart, he accepted my remarriage and a new father figure in his life, at a time when he desperately needed one. This was a new role for Larry as well, because he had never been a dad before.

Not only did Larry ask Tyler's permission to marry me, but he also asked Tyler to be his best man at the wedding. Tyler excitedly accepted his invitation. That was when I asked my son to honor me by walking me down the aisle and giving me away, as he was to stand next to his soon-to-be dad.

Larry was working a lot during that time, and he told Tyler and me to go and look at wedding rings. We did so, and it did not take long for Tyler and me to find the perfect one. When Larry was off work the next time, he and I went. I told him the price range and the store. He searched and found the same exact one. I knew then it was meant for us to be together. I cannot explain it; I just knew.

Tyler mentioned that he felt that his daddy helped pick Larry out. Tyler imagined that his daddy was standing up in heaven next to Jesus. Jesus would point out certain men, and Stan would say, "No, Lord, that one doesn't have broad enough shoulders to put up with Elaine's crap." (Please remember that these were the words of a thirteen-year-old boy.) Stan helped Jesus pick Larry out for us, for a new phase of our lives that he himself was not destined to share.

We announced our engagement to Larry's mother and daddy first. Then, that Sunday, Larry decided it was time to join the church, so Tyler made sure he was there with us. (He usually went to another Sunday school class.) Larry's brother Terry was a deacon at the church, and Tyler told him that Larry was going to join. Tyler did not tell him about the engagement; he only said that Larry was going to join the church that morning. Terry made sure that he was the one to greet Larry when we walked down for his decision. It was not until Terry looked over at my hand that he had any idea that we had gotten engaged. Terry whispered to me, and I told him that the wedding was set for October 27. It came time for Terry to introduce his brother as a new member of the church. He did so with tears in his eyes, because his family had prayed for Larry to accept Jesus back into his life and become active in church.

I never made demands on Larry. (Well, except for insisting that he get a complete physical before the wedding if he wanted me to marry him; I didn't want to get into another "bad heart" situation!) His coming back to the Lord and the church was all of his own free will. As Terry was expressing his love for his brother to the congregation, Tyler and I were standing up with him. Terry then announced that he had just found out that his brother was engaged to Elaine Knight. Everyone knew me as "the widow woman."

The news came as a complete surprise (or even a shock) to almost everyone, because no one really knew that I was dating, much less getting married. I had already told my Sunday school class that morning, and they could not have been happier for me. I had told them that I was going to need their help in planning a wedding, because I had no family left—only them. As Terry was telling the congregation about our engagement, I looked out and saw Terry's wife, and her mouth dropped in utter amazement and shock.

Larry and I began to plan our wedding and our honeymoon. We decided to have a formal wedding because neither of us had done that the first time around. When I had married Stan, it had been on a lake in Tyler, Texas, and Daddy had walked me down a garden path to the lake so we could be united. Larry's first marriage had been in someone's home. This time, I needed to set an example for my son and to figure out ways to honor him in the ceremony.

We had not expected that September 11, 2001, would happen. How uncertain the world was at that time. The event threw uncertainty into our future together. As the events of that day unfolded, I knew the ministry would be growing, because there were going to be so many new widows from just that day alone. September 11 affected our honeymoon, because we didn't know if we would be able to go on our cruise to the Bahamas. We had already paid for the trip, and we were told that we could not get credit for it, much less postpone it. This began a whole new idea of having to get our wills in order, and so on, in case anything were to happen—if we decided to go.

In September, I had a widows' meeting at Rosann and Pete's home, a historic Victorian home that was to be the site of my wedding reception in just a few short weeks. The widows turned it into a shower for me, and I never felt so loved as I did at that time. It had only been months before that Mother had died, and I felt alone. But all of that diminished when I began to feel just how much these ladies appreciated the ministry—doing this for me.

That was when I realized so many things about my life. Some of my why questions had been answered. I was living in total faith, like I had never done before.

Our wedding day came. My friend Cyndy and her family had traveled from Texas the day before. Cyndy and Doyle were the only ones to be present at both of my weddings, since so many people had gone home to be with the Lord since the first one. Larry, Tyler, and I met them for breakfast that morning. We had gotten them tickets to the Grand Ole Opry for the night before, and they came into the restaurant totally decked out in their souvenirs and talked constantly about the fun time they'd had and how beautiful Nashville was.

We spent a couple of hours with them. Cyndy made the comment that I wasn't the same anymore. This was the first time we were together since before Stan's death. I told her that the death of your spouse does something to you, and you are not the same person as before. I told her I hoped that I was a better person for learning how to include joy in my life and to move on. They loved Larry and commented on how much he and Stan were alike. They knew, without a doubt, that I was happy.

Larry, Tyler, and I went to the apartment and began to get ready. The three of us drove over to the church together. We did not give in to the superstition that it is bad luck for the groom to see the bride until the ceremony. (We are still happily married today.)

We got to the church and walked around the sanctuary to see how things were progressing. Tyler helped out as best he could. He looked so handsome. He was dressed in a black suit, with a black shirt, and a silver tie. We'd had his hair frosted that week, and it was spiked up. He was so excited about the new life we were starting. He could have made it very difficult for us. When Larry had asked his permission to marry me, I had told Tyler that if he had any reservations at all he should speak up, and I would honor his decision. But he just loved Larry from the beginning because Larry included him in everything.

Larry was also wearing a black suit: the first suit he had worn in many, many years. He had on a silver, silky pullover shirt. (I didn't make him wear a tie.) He was so handsome, with his silver hair and that sweet grin, particularly when you saw the dimple!

Some of my friends came into the bride's room to give me hugs and to support me because it was difficult for me, not having my parents there with me. Daddy would have loved Larry very much. Daddy had always been protective of me, as daddies should be. But he would have approved.

Peggy came in, helped me into my dress, and fixed my hair. Then Tyler came in to tell me it was time. All of a sudden, I was filled with nervousness. I knew that I wanted to marry Larry, but it was the first time I realized that I was embarking on a new phase of my life, and that Stan clearly was not part of it.

Tyler took me by the arm, and we walked down the aisle together as the music played. I looked over at my sweet and handsome son, and he was smiling from ear to ear. Oh, how wonderful God was to us on this day. I praised him right then for my son. I was thankful for all we had gone through together—the good and the bad—because I could see the happiness on his face, the way it was at that moment.

I looked over, and there was Kitty. When I think of the word *grace,* Kitty's face comes to mind. She had been such an inspiration to me. She sat in the pew where my mother would have sat.

As we made our way down the aisle, I looked over at Peggy. How big her smile was, and how blessed I was with her present at yet another first! Then I looked into the face of my husband-to-be, and the tears began to flow—not because I did not want to go through with this, but because I was happy. I never had thought I would be doing this again at this particular point in my life.

As I got to the end of the pews, I had a rose for Kitty, who was as close as a mother to me. When Larry and I walked back down the aisle after we were wed, I had another rose to give to his mother, with a hug. This was something I had done in my first wedding, and I wanted to make the same kind of tribute in this one.

Larry took my hand as Tyler gave me away, and he looked down at me with his gentle smile. I began to cry, and continued to cry through the service. Peggy sang for us, and it could not have been any more precious than this.

We had added a part to the ceremony without telling Tyler. I had found a necklace with three rings on it. The rings represented the three of us. Our pastor incorporated the necklace into the ceremony, so that it was not just about Larry and me, it was about joining the family together as one; no one would feel left out. The smile on Tyler's face was worth more to me than anything else in that entire ceremony. Even Peggy was fighting the tears and, at the same time, trying to get Tyler to stop playing with his necklace during the service. (I said it was precious, not perfect!)

Normally when you are wed, you turn around and are introduced as Mr. and Mrs. Somebody. The three of us were introduced as the Cook family. My advice to any young widow out there with children is to be sure to incorporate your children in all facets of the wedding. Give them responsibilities; let them be a part of it. There is no job too small or too large for them to do, if you want the blending of your families to move smoothly and for everyone to feel a part of it. To this day, Tyler often mentions how much he appreciated us including him from the very beginning. I know that it is one of the main reasons why he has been so accepting and happy. He has felt the love of our marriage surround him and include him in every way. (Well, maybe not in *everything!*)

October 27 turned out to be a very cold day, and of course, my wedding dress was not made for the cold weather. The dress, believe it or not, was white, long, and formal. I was a widow, so I felt that white was appropriate. Again, it was an example I was setting for Tyler because one day he would find his bride, and he would have that experience to draw upon.

We stayed around for the pictures, and then headed over to Rosann and Pete's home for our reception. Their home was beautifully decorated, and what a feeling it was to walk in and see all of our loved ones there. I went around (still in my long dress and still cold) to greet every one of our guests. My new mother-in-law said later that I had blown her friends away, because this was about Larry and me and I had taken the time to greet everyone that had come.

We got ready to leave. Praise God, I was able to change back into something warmer! I hugged Tyler as he talked with his new family members. He was going to stay with some friends when we went on our honeymoon. We said our good-byes, and off we went to begin our new life as husband and wife.

It hit me later that evening just what starting a new life together meant. I had finally gotten comfortable with Stan and had trained him to be a good husband! (Ha.) But now, here I was, thirty-nine years old and starting all over again.

Larry and I went out for a special dinner. Then retired to our hotel room, because we were flying out to Florida very early the next morning so we could catch our cruise. I was not expecting to feel the way I did that night. Larry, bless his heart, was very patient and sweet. We were being intimate, and I began to cry. I don't know if it was because it was something special for two people starting their lives together, or if I was feeling guilty for being intimate with someone besides Stan. But Larry handled it very well, and he couldn't have been more of a gentleman than he was that night.

The next morning, we got up early and began our cruise to the Bahamas. We enjoyed every moment of it. (Well, except for the times we got seasick.) It was strange because, since it wasn't too long after September 11, we had to go through all sorts of security procedures. As we left the harbor, we had military helicopters surrounding us for the longest time.

We got back from our cruise, and Larry wanted us to rest for the afternoon. He wanted to check Tyler out of school early the next day and take him on the rest of the honeymoon with us: to Dollywood in the Smoky Mountains of Tennessee.

Tyler was excited when we got home, and we told him what the next day was going to bring. We gave him his presents from the Bahamas, told him about the trip, and, of course, I told him how much I had missed him.

The next morning, I got Tyler off to school. When he was gone, I began to pack a bag for him. After a couple of hours, we went to his school and checked him out. We would not tell him where we were going; we just said that Larry wanted to take him on a trip so he could share in part of the honeymoon with us.

When we arrived in Pigeon Forge, we told him about the planned weekend, and I knew right then that we had done the right thing by including him in some way. I told Tyler that all of this was Larry's idea (which it was). This was how our family began to fit together perfectly.

My marriage to Larry has been a blessed gift from God. It has not taken away from my marriage to Stan, but life does go on. I am so grateful to have enough love in my heart for these two wonderful men. I have truly been blessed to be loved by two men and to have had two beautiful marriages. Most people cannot say they found that the first time, if at all.

The relationship that Larry and Tyler have is absolutely remarkable. Tyler could have resented Larry in every way—Mom would have to share her time with both. Larry could have been resentful because he had never had to "share" someone before, and all of a sudden, to have a teenager—that can be overwhelming. But God has been present in all of our lives through this whole relationship-building process.

In the time we have been together, there has only been one incident when Tyler and Larry shared words and I had to break it up. It was hard because Larry was trying to discipline Tyler. But he was going about it the wrong way and accused me of being too soft on him. I told Larry that I knew my son inside and out. I knew what made him tick, and I knew what would be detrimental to his confidence.

I had a long talk with Larry about parenthood, telling him times have changed since we were kids. When we were Tyler's age, we didn't have to deal with life the way Tyler has, who had lost so many loved ones by the time he was twelve. I had a long talk with Tyler and explained that Larry loved him, but the only parenting he had to go by was the way he had been raised. I told him that Larry wanted him to succeed more than he did.

It took a while to get them both over their falling out, but the important thing is that they did, and they have learned from it. It has not happened again. When Larry disagrees with an action of Tyler's, he is more willing to try to listen and to understand. And Tyler has a lot of respect for Larry—and for the dad he has become.

6

The Life of a Child

At the time of this writing, Tyler is seventeen years old and soon to be a senior in high school. The relationship that Tyler and Larry have today is one for which I am so very grateful to our Lord, Jesus Christ—for being present through those difficult times as well as the not-so-difficult times. There is no power struggle among us. Tyler knows the limits, and I have tried to teach him right from wrong. Tyler knows that if he makes a wrong choice, there will be consequences for it. But Tyler also knows that whether his decisions are good or bad, Larry and I are going to be there for him. He knows we are going to be there to cheer him on and to help him pick up the pieces, because we love him unconditionally, as God loves us.

It took a long time for me to realize that Tyler changed after Stan died. I do not know why I didn't think he should. After all, I changed. But Tyler had always been involved in baseball and Boy Scouts, and I was beginning to realize that these were things he didn't enjoy any longer. He had been doing them because it was something he and his daddy used to do together, but when Stan was no longer there, Tyler lost interest in them.

It took a long time for me to realize what Tyler's gifts were. I knew he was sensitive and compassionate toward others, but after Stan's death, he became even more sensitive, and needed even more to feel as if he fit in. I also realized that he needed to experience being his own person. He has a talent for art, drawing, and music.

Tyler has a way with people. He can make you feel as if you are the most important person as he talks with you, and he can do this with people from all walks of life. He has a smile that can melt my heart with just a glance. We even have a secret "I love you" sign, so that when he is in a crowd of teens we can make this gesture, and no one knows what it means but us.

I love sharing in Tyler's life. He has his friends, but he always comes home with a smile on his face. I take pride in that, because if God had not loved us through these times of difficulty, I am not sure we would have the relationship we share. God uses difficult circumstances to bring people close together. There is a natural bond between mothers and sons anyway, and, when you add all of the tragedies we have gone through together, you can't help but build a stronger bond. Tyler also had a very special bond with his daddy. The two of them were inseparable. Whatever Stan was doing, Tyler was right there. Whatever Tyler wanted to do, Stan was there to be supportive and to be a part of it in any way he could.

The relationship that Tyler and I had in his early years had been very good. Stan was older and had waited a long time to become a father, but I hadn't been particularly interested in growing up, getting married, or having children. But I am so thankful that I did, because I have lived a complete life in so many ways. Tyler knows that I will always be there for him, even if he has done wrong. I praise God for that.

Tyler has learned a few things from his dad that I would rather he hadn't learned, but I have had the past few years to help mold him into a man that will be a wonderful and caring husband and will adore his children. Stan also taught him how to be a good man as well, but Stan was not perfect and I have made many mistakes with Tyler in the past few years. The most trouble occurred after Stan's death, when he went through the phase of stealing, failing school, and so on.

The one thing that hurt me tremendously was when Tyler became interested in pornography. And that was also one of the things that his dad had done that had hurt me in more ways than I can express. When I caught Tyler, it was more than just the usual kind of "interested to see what it is" sort of thing. We discussed it, and I told him how morally wrong and degrading to women it was, and that he was being disrespectful. Because of our enormous conversations about it, it is something he is not interested in now. But it was a concern back then. Now my concern is that he is in between being a boy and being a man. But I have to have trust that he picked up on a few things and will think things through and pray for answers. He is so much wiser than I was at his age, but he has been through so much more than I could have imagined at that point in my life as well.

There are things that I am concerned about regarding my son, but every parent has concerns for the future of their children. I have prayed for many years for Tyler's bride and for his future children. I have prayed for his health. But what I pray for most is his relationship with Jesus Christ. I want to see him grow and flourish in God's word. These are the areas of great concern for me right now, but I see hope in him at the same time that I see the struggles he faces.

Tyler is currently into music that I do not understand. He wants to pierce portions of his body that I cannot imagine. And he is into this new "straight-edge" way of life that has me concerned. Straight-edge means they are abstinent until marriage, and they do not do drugs or use alcohol—but they question God and need proof of his existence. Tyler does go to church every Sunday, and he is the one who insists that we go, for which I praise God. If I had to drag him there, then I would know that he wasn't fighting Satan, and this way I know he is. It is comforting to know that Tyler hasn't given up completely.

I am proud of my son and proud that he has overcome so many things. He enjoys being around his mom, and every once in a while, we get to go out on a date together, just the two of us. I feel blessed as I watch him grow into a man, using his compassion and endurance to help others. Tyler is like me: he can single out an individual who is hurting. He might not know why they are hurting, but he knows there is something, and he befriends them and makes them feel comfortable and important. Not many teenagers can do that, but then, there are not many adults who can do that either—to be in tune with others and not really know about it or understand it.

7

Finding Purpose and Leaping into Faith

For the first time in my life, I finally see the purpose of all I have endured with God's amazing grace. I have compassion for others who are hurting. Not necessarily just widows, but all hearts. I have a sense about people; I can look into a crowd of faces and sense they are hurting. I do not know the hurt they are experiencing, but I feel their hurt. I often speak to various groups about grief or similar topics, and I look across the room and can just feel the looks on their faces by searching their hearts. I cannot explain it. Some often refer to it as the gift of discernment. I often refer to it as a curse, because, after I experience that, it drains me emotionally and physically. But I feel that God uses those times to keep me fresh and true to my feelings and where they come from, in order to help others.

The calling in my life is to minister to those who are hurting, particularly widows. Widows are often left in a black hole in our churches and communities. The pastors, deacons, and elders really don't know what to do with us after the first couple of months. They mean well, but how can they minister to the hearts and the spiritual growth of widows if they do not understand?

That is where the ministry of Widow2Widow (W2W) comes in. W2W picks up where the leaders of the church leave off. Only another widow will understand the needs of other widows. There is nothing more comforting to a new widow than having a "journeyed" widow become her mentor. The "journeyed" widow has so much to offer, and the new widow eventually begins to open up and know she can share things that she normally cannot.

Our families and friends expect us to be back to normal after the first couple of months. We want to be back to normal as well. But what we have to learn—along with everyone else—is that we have to find a whole new way of being normal, because the way we have known no longer exists, since the other half of us is now gone. It takes time to find a whole new self alone. It takes time to find purpose in our lives again. It takes time to grieve. That is something that cannot be rushed, but it is needed in order for us to move on.

God's promises to us are real, but we have to be open to them and to search his Word for them, and we need a ministry like W2W that will show us how to do this and to feel again. We think that we will never experience joy and happiness again. But there is a difference between joy and happiness. Joy is a gift from God. It is always there, but because happiness is based on circumstances, we sometimes lump the two together. We know the joy of God through our relationship with him. Happiness will come and go, but joy will remain, if you will seek it and allow it into your life.

When a woman is widowed, she not only loses her life-mate, but she also loses a part of her identity in the process. Sometimes she loses friends as well, because they don't understand. These are all things that we learn to grieve in the process. It is not easy, but it is something we must all do in order to see the full picture of what God has in store for our lives.

It is difficult when you have friends who are a couple; most likely they will invite you out to dinner, but you are the "third wheel." It hurts to see your friends as couples together, but they are also strained in this new relationship because they have lost a friend and are not sure how to treat you. Sometimes our friends feel threatened because they think that being in association with you might cause the same reality to hit their lives.

There is so much more to being a widow than just the loss of a husband. Everything changes, even relationships. But God knows all of that, and he holds a special place for us during this time. He will place others in our paths who will help fill some voids, but our relationship with him is to be complete. He wants to be our husband.

God has called widows for a special purpose. We are to hold a special place in the church as women of prayer. We are called to pray because we have a special bond with God; his Word states that we should be in prayer for all things, and that the church should recognize the widow for this purpose. In I Timothy 5:5-6, The widow who is really in need and left all alone puts her hope in God and continues night and day to pray and to ask God for help. 6.) But the widow who lives for pleasure is dead even while she lives. (NIV)

But the church does not always see that. They feel we need to have socials, like having a Christmas dinner hosted by the deacons and their wives. Those are very nice gestures, but do they really solve our hurts? No, only being with others on this journey and knowing we are not alone helps. We need to share in true laughter and to cry freely, without feeling guilty or embarrassed.

We have to give ourselves permission to feel again. Why doesn't it just come naturally? Because we, as women, are not wired to do so.

The ministry goes out and educates others about our needs as widows. How many times have you been told to call someone in particular if you are in need of anything? Do they really think we will ask for help? Sometimes we do, but most of the time we will either do without or figure it out on our own. That is okay, except that perhaps we are telling them not to do something God has encouraged them to do. I have told others that if they feel something needs to be done, they should do it. Do not ask us if it is okay; just do it, because we would more than likely say no anyway. It is hard to be on the receiving end sometimes, isn't it?

I know that when Stan died, I never thought about eating. I could remember that my son needed to eat, but rarely would I remember that I had not eaten in several days—literally! Within seven months, I had lost over one hundred pounds. I was a big girl and needed to lose the weight, but not eating was an area where I felt I was in control. Part of it was a sacrifice, because food and money were not plentiful with Stan's untimely death and no insurance to carry us through. I did not make enough money to cover the rent, insurance, car payments, and so forth. It was my controlling attitude that said it was okay for me not to eat because I was in control of so few things! I still have health problems today because of that situation, but God used many others to make me see that I was unhealthy and losing weight. These people knew that I was lying if I told them everything was okay. I was not okay in any form or fashion, but I was not sharing that with strangers. But God had people send us money, or talk to the church about what they felt our situation was. The benevolence committee paid some major bills for us about six months into our journey, they gave us grocery gift certificates so we could purchase food to have in the house, and helped in other things as we needed them.

None of this was easy for me. I was never a very gracious receiver, and, to this day, it is hard for me to look some of those people in the eye—people that I know were instrumental in those early months of recovery for Tyler and me.

8

The Fellowship of Widows

There are many misconceptions of widows. First, everyone believes that only an elderly lady can be a widow. Secondly, they think all widows are left wealthy. I fit neither of those misconceptions. A third misconception is that widows are constantly sorrowful. Excuse me, but yes, I have had a time of being sorrowful, which is part of the grieving process. But does that mean we have to remain in sorrow for the rest of our lives? I know that is something Stan would not have wanted me to do for a long period of time. There are still days that I miss him terribly and want to share with him, but that doesn't mean that my life is filled with sorrow.

I am going to share with you some of the stories of women who crossed my path in the early days of our ministry, before it became known to other churches and grew into its own nonprofit agency.

I spoke earlier about my young widow, Letty. Letty holds a very special place in my heart, partly because of her acceptance of Christ into her life, and I was blessed to be a part of that. But Letty had many struggles to overcome. Since she was Hispanic and her in-laws were Caucasian, there were struggles about how Letty's son, Austin, was to be raised. Austin is a wonderful boy: loving, handsome, and well-mannered. Letty made some mistakes along the way, mostly by allowing the in-laws to raise Austin after her husband's death. Sometimes there can be too much help. But when Letty reached a point in her life where she felt she needed to move on, it was difficult for the in-laws to accept. They wanted her to be happy, but they were afraid she would take Austin away from them. Ultimately, the relationship became very strained, particularly when Letty began to date again and found a new husband and family who understood the struggles she had undergone. Letty married a young Hispanic pastor who was a widower and had children of his own. They blended their families into one. It has been very difficult for the original in-laws. Austin was caught in the middle and was now being raised in the environment in which his mom had grown up.

Each of us makes mistakes, and I could see them on both sides, because I was an outsider. I couldn't say too much, but I did share some points of view that I wish I hadn't because I don't think they made much of a difference. However, defending Letty and her actions—she needed to move on. Perhaps she didn't make some wise choices along the way, but they are choices she had to live with, and she is very happy now in her new marriage.

Letty and I spoke once about how different intimacy is with a new husband and how guilty we were when we first remarried. The part that is so wonderful is that, if this ministry did not exist and these relationships hadn't been formed, there would never have been the opportunity to share anything with anyone. We have to share with those who will understand and tell us the truth, not just pacify us and tell us what we want to hear.

Let me tell you about another widow. We must have been in our second year of the ministry, because at the time, we held our meetings in the gym area of our old church. We had a speaker talk to the ladies about "Organization 101," and it was really interesting how the ladies took in all of the tips the woman shared.

A few days before this meeting, a woman had called me and told me that her father had recently died. They were in the process of getting her mother moved to Tennessee from New York, and her mother did not know anyone here. She had asked me a lot of questions about the ministry and had been very interested in having her mother attend, but her mother would not come alone. I had encouraged her to come with her mother. I always encouraged friends, siblings, and children to come to the meetings, particularly if it was the first time for the widow, because it is alarming to walk into a room of strangers.

I had told the daughter what to expect, which was that Nita (the mother) would be welcomed with a hug and would have a mentor "adopt" her and sit with her at the meeting. We always have times of fellowship, and there would be some time to bond.

They came in, and Nita was very feeble-looking and obviously did not want to be there. I sat her down with Tommye, and we began the meeting. As our speaker was going over her agenda, Nita was just in tears. I had told her daughter that when we need to cry at these meetings, we do so. No one ever feels ashamed of releasing their emotions, whether with tears or with laughter.

I was in the back of the room, and some of the ladies were unsure about what to do for Nita. I moved to where Nita was sitting and sat behind her. I gave her tissues, and just kept my hand on her shoulder, caressing and patting it to let her know it was okay and that she was not alone.

Nita returned, and, once she got settled in after her final move from New York, she had already begun a friendship with Tommye. As God had planned all along, Nita ended up moving into the same retirement facility where Tommye and some of the other ladies were living.

There has been a complete change in Nita; she found a best friend in Tommye, and they are very good for one another. Nita cares for Tommye, now that Tommye's health has deteriorated, and even Nita's health isn't the best. But watching these women together, you would think they had been friends for most of their lives. It has only been maybe three to four years. Again, if it wasn't for the ministry, how else would these women's lives be touched in such a special way? How else would they be able to share their hearts for others to witness?

Another lady is Peggy L. Peggy L.had been widowed in January 2004. Our paths did not cross until about four days before the retreat in September that year. She was so lost. It amazes me to see how God placed her on my path and in this ministry because by the time she returned home, she had changed into a woman who had hope and was able to comfort others as she herself had been comforted.

Peggy L. was an introvert. She stayed within her shell and came out only when she felt forced to. Well, that was the old Peggy L. This woman has changed so much. Now she realizes her calling in life, which has given her a new sense of purpose since the death of her husband, Bobby.

Peggy L. never would have thought she had the courage within her to board a bus filled with ladies she did not know and go to a retreat for widows that she did not care to be a part of, but the Holy Spirit would not leave her and kept pressing on her heart that this was what she was to do.

Whenever a widow signed up for the retreat and needed to room with someone else, I would pray earnestly for the right roommate, particularly since I did not know all of these women. When Peggy L's registration came in, I prayed and prayed to find out who her roommate should be. Never did I imagine that God had a special someone who would help her in so many ways. That woman was Carol Marie. I had spoken to Carol Marie on the phone, but I had not met her personally. For a couple of weeks prior to the retreat, I had moved one woman after another from rooming with Carol Marie, and it wasn't until Peggy came into the picture that I realized that these two were meant to share their time together at the retreat.

This has been a major inspiration, because these two ladies have formed such a great friendship. There is nothing better than to have relationships that happen because of God's love for us and his desire to see us grow.

For Peggy L., Carol Marie has been an answer to prayer. On the first night, after all of the events, Carol Marie gave Peggy L. a foot massage. I won't tell you about my reaction the next morning, I was happy for Peggy L., but hey! I was the one that had put them together! On the second night, another Peggy R.(who was rooming with me) went to their room because she and Carol Marie had a lot in common: makeup, fashion, all the girly stuff. While the three of them were in the room, Carol Marie gave Peggy L. the ultimate makeover (which is her specialty). Peggy R. came back to our room and said that I wouldn't believe the transformation I was going to see the next day.

The next morning, Peggy L. came to breakfast; she was looking down at her feet as she walked in. Carol Marie had cut and styled her hair, and I don't think any of us were prepared for what would unfold in the months to come. Peggy L. began to come out of her shell and explore the visions that God was giving her during her time of grief.

When Peggy L. had come to my attention before the retreat, she had told me what church she belonged to. I actually knew her pastor well, from my days of working at the Tennessee Baptist Convention. I had called her pastor and told him that he had needs within his congregation that concerned the widows, and we had talked for a very long time. He had known that I had a widows' ministry but had never thought about the needs within his own church—they had needed to be pointed out to him.

Peggy L. is now the group leader for their church in the Widow2Widow ministry, and she has been blossoming like a beautiful rose, into one of God's major creations. She has since resigned her position at the school in which she was a staff member in order to fulfill what she feels God is leading her to do, which is to minister to those who are hurting.

9

Sorrow and Grief Explained

I am reminded of the words of the hymn, "It Is Well with My Soul":

When sorrows like sea billows roll—

Whatever my lot

Thou hast taught me to say,

It is well, it is well, with my soul.

Sorrow is our natural response to trials. It is a time for us to go to God in prayer and thank him for loving us so much that we experience these times of trials, so that we may grow closer to him and see the picture of what he has planned for our lives—whether here on earth, or for the glory of his kingdom.

In James 1:2–12, it is stated that we should "consider it pure joy…whenever (we) face trials of many kinds." Why is this? Trials are seldom met with joy. However, James not only instructs us to face trials with joy, but with pure joy. He is telling us not to fake joy. Don't you find it important that this is listed before James 1:27, which talks about caring for widows and orphans??

One of the most fulfilling ways of dealing with my own pain has been in founding Widow2Widow™. It is an opportunity to reach out to others in pain, and to encourage them and help them understand that God will turn their tragedies into triumphs.

Praise is the distinctive word *bless*. When the Lord blesses us, by knowing what our needs are and then responds to them; we bless the Lord, by accepting his virtues and respond to them.

One of the things I have learned to do is to help leaders of our groups understand the importance of ministering through spiritual gifts. We all have gifts that God has given to us. And over time and through our life experiences, our gifts may shift somewhat, in order that we may proceed in the right direction. God leads us on specific paths as we grow in our spiritual walks with him. We all need to recognize personal gifts and to use them in order to further his kingdom.

According to Paul, there are seven gifts given for ministry purposes. Our gifts differ according to the grace that is given to us; let us use them. Romans 12:6–8 lists the gifts that Paul has identified:

1. prophecy

2. ministering, which also may be referred to as service

3. teaching

4. exhortation

5. giving

6. leading, which also may be called administration or organization

7. mercy

Paul states that each person has one of these gifts set apart for just him or her. God is the giver of the gifts, and, through the Holy Spirit, he is the one who helps us identify, develop, and use our gifts. These are not gifts that we "work up" or that we have the privilege to choose for ourselves. They are gifts of God to us. We must recognize how we are made, embrace our own gifts, and then seek to grow in them.

I admit it: I wish I had the gift of teaching, but I don't. However, that does not mean that I cannot teach. What I have found is that we each must find our own gifts, and there are Bible studies to show us how to do that. It is important that we allow the Holy Spirit to move within us. We must work toward recognizing what is in our lives and seek to grow in the Word for a relationship with Jesus Christ.

As widows, we have so much on our shoulders. But we hold a special place in God's eyes, and it even says in the Bible many times that no one is to take advantage of us or harm us. But we are also to spend our lives in service to him in whatever way he puts in our hearts, and the only way to do so is to study his word, to talk with others, and to pray.

When I was a new widow, none of this came to my mind. It wasn't until later that I understood the vision that God had given me. Even now I do not understand all that I can see, but I am stepping out in faith, trusting God, and doing what he is asking me to do. Does that mean I make the right choices? No. Sometimes—most of the time—I go with the desires of my heart, and, as much as I would like to make the right choices, they aren't always what God desires for me. Life has always been complicated hasn't it?

Jan Dravecky wrote the following:

A ministry of love based on Romans 12:9–21

> I am amazed at what God had to take me through in order to change me from one who avoided suffering people to someone who is able to comfort those who are in pain and distress. He had to take me through a tremendous amount of pain to prepare me for this ministry to comfort. He had to change my heart. I don't know exactly how he did it or when he did it, but I can tell you where he did it—in the valley of suffering. We didn't orchestrate any of this; we didn't even welcome it at the time. We have known the fellowship of suffering. Joined the ranks of all those who became useful to God through the things that they suffered. (Excerpt from the *NIV Encouragement Bible: The Answer for Those Who Hurt.*)

I am thankful for so much. My fifth-grade teacher, Nadine, who I mentioned earlier, has shared many things with me, but one scripture verse in particular that I share with others is Ecclesiastes 1:18: "For with much wisdom comes much sorrow; the more knowledge, the more grief." (NIV) This sums up my life when I think about it sometimes. Many times I have suffered the loss of a loved one or the loss of something that meant a great deal to me. I have grieved over many things that were important to my life. Because of it I have grown and survived by the grace of God, who entrusts me with bits and pieces, knowing that I can't handle it all at one time.

The Ecclesiastes book of the *Encouragement Bible* has so many wonderful and encouraging writings that go along with the Scriptures. In reference to Ecclesiastes 2:15–16: "Then I thought in my heart, 'The fate of the fool will overtake me also. What then do I gain by being wise?' I said in my heart, 'This too is meaningless.' For the wise man, like the fool, will not be long remembered; in days to come both will be forgotten. Like the fool, the wise man too must die!"

In reference to this Scripture, Solomon was right when he declared, "Like the fool, the wise man too must die!" (Ecclesiastes 2:16). But that is where the similarities end, for the life of the righteous doesn't end at death. Joseph S. Flacks, a devoted Christian of the past generation, understood this well. He prepared a special postcard to be mailed to his friends upon his death. On August 14, 1940, he died, and the cards were dated and sent out. Joseph's message read:

Triumphant Through Grace

- This is to announce: I moved out of the old mud house (2 Corinthians 5:1).

- Arrived in Glory-land instantly in the charge of an angelic escort (Luke 16:22).

- Absent from the body, at home with the Lord (2 Corinthians 5:6)

- I find as foretold (Psalm 16:11) in His presence fullness of joy…pleasures forevermore!

- Will look for you on the way up at the redemption of the body (Romans 8:23). Till then, look up!

Isn't that a wonderful way to look at eternity and to share the Word with our family and friends? What legacy will I leave on this earth when it is my time to arrive in the "Glory-land"? What may I do now to be effective for the glory of God's kingdom?

Read the book of Ecclesiastes and put your hope in God. Life is uncertain, but if you put your hope in God, he will carry you through all circumstances. God has given us just enough wisdom to realize how little we know. He has "set eternity in the hearts of men; yet they cannot fathom what God has done from beginning to end" (Ecclesiastes 3:11).

We cannot predict the day of our passing (Ecclesiastes 8:8). We cannot know what will happen on this earth after we depart (Ecclesiastes 3:22). In fact, "No one can comprehend what goes under the sun. Despite all efforts to search it out, man cannot discover its meaning. Even if a wise man claims he knows, he cannot really comprehend it" (Ecclesiastes 8:17).

We do not know what will happen next year, next week, or even in the next hour. We do not know which of our ideas or enterprises may succeed or fail (Ecclesiastes 11:6). We do not know what wars or natural disasters may wait around the corner (Ecclesiastes 1–2). Look at the tsunami in December 2004 in Asia, and the many thousands of people who are missing and dead. Think about the events that unfolded on September 11, 2001, and the fear many experienced before their untimely deaths.

What is the answer to living in such uncertainty? "Remember your Creator in the days of your youth, before the days of trouble came and the years approach when you will say, 'I find no pleasure in them'" (Ecclesiastes 12:1). The bottom line, then, is this: "Fear God and keep his commandments. For this is the whole duty of man" (Ecclesiastes 12:13).

When we are stricken with some great hardship or trial and we don't know which way to turn, it's paramount to remember the words of Jeremiah 10:23: "I know, O Lord, that a man's life is not his own; it is not for man to direct his steps."

The worst thing we can do in times of trouble is to act rashly, to take whatever course of action seems easiest at the time. We must remember that our lives is not our own, and that God has promised to lead us.

Sometimes that leadership isn't at all clear. That's when we wait for him to take us by the hand, and, in his time, bring us into the light.

Joni Eareckson Tada wrote a commentary in the *Encouragement Bible* called, "Why, Lord?" She states:

> God's plan is specific. He doesn't say, "Into each life a little rain must fall," then aim a hose in earth's general direction to see who gets the wettest. He doesn't reach for a key, wind up nature with its sunny days and hurricanes, then sit back and watch the show. He doesn't let Satan prowl about totally unrestricted. He doesn't believe in a hands-off policy of governing. He's not our planet's absentee landlord. Rather, he screens the trials that come to each of us—allowing only those that accomplish his good plan, because he takes no joy in human agony. These trials aren't evenly distributed from person to person. This can discourage us, for we are not privy to his reasons. But, in God's wisdom and love, every trial in a Christian's life is ordained from eternity past, custom-made for that believer's eternal good, even when it doesn't seem like it. Nothing happens by accident, not even tragedy. Not even sins committed against us.
>
> No one can do without hope. It is the one thing in all our distress that can keep us afloat. And hope is built on instances of past grace. Gregory of Nissa has the following words to encourage your own heart to rejoice in hope: "Hope always draws the soul from the beauty that is seen to what is beyond, always rekindles the desires for the hidden through what is perceived." *(By Steve Halliday, Zondervan Corporation)*
>
> "The Calvary road with Jesus is not a joyless road. It is a painful one, but it is a profoundly happy one. The happiest people in the world are the people who experience the mystery of "Christ in (them), the hope of glory" (Colossians 1:27), satisfying their deep longings and freeing them to extend the afflictions of Christ through their own sufferings to the world." *(John Piper, from "Desiring God", Tenth Anniversary Edition)*
>
> God really does comfort his children—and most often he chooses to do so through the arms and legs and voices and ears and faces and tears of men and women who have been to the front lines and returned with battle scars (2 Corinthians 1:3–4). Someone who has "been there" has the credibility and the understanding to know what it is that the person in pain is going

through—the questions, the doubts, the fears. They can speak both compassionately and authoritatively because of their own experience.

I wonder—have you considered how God might want to use you to comfort someone in pain? "But I'm in pain myself," you reply. Yes, but who better to reach out with understanding, empathy, and genuine concern? If you have suffered and God has stepped in with his comfort, then you qualify to join his army of comforters. I hope you are ready to enlist because we need you. And so does a hurting world.

This is the basis for Widow2Widow and what it means to others who are on this journey. Won't you support the ministry, either financially, in prayer, or by helping to lead a group to minister to widows across our country?

10

The Journey of Widowhood and Purpose

It is stated in Scripture that as widows, we are called to prayer. In the book, *The Transforming Power of Prayer: Deepening Your Friendship with God,* James Houston states that prayer is wider than the world, deeper than the heart, and older than the origin of humanity—because prayer originates from the very character of God.

We pray not simply to enjoy the experience of praying, but to communicate with God, to submit to him, to be like him, to love and serve him. Prayer is much more than just a challenge. Prayer is our response to God's interest in us and his love for us. To pray is to become aware that God's spirit lives within us. Through prayer, we explore a deeper and more intimate relationship with God.

Jesus stands outside, asking us to open the doors of our hearts to him. This willingness to open ourselves to God is where all true prayer begins. Once we have learned to respond to God in this way, by saying, "Yes, Lord, come into my life to stay," then we can begin to focus our attention on him.

To be robbed of our own willpower may seem a shocking indignity and deprivation, so we struggle to avoid it. However, when we place ourselves entirely in God's hands, we discover—to our surprise—that we have not been robbed or violated but given a new freedom and joy in life. It is only when we are "in Christ," receiving the power of God's spirit, that we can live new lives.

Prayer makes us more flexible before God. We become open to his spirit, begin to respond to what we read about in the Bible, and become curious about how he wants our lives to be. Prayer becomes more of a matter of listening than talking. It is obvious that he has much more to say to us than we can bear at any one time.

There are many ways we can encourage our growth in prayer. The most important thing we need to do to help ourselves in prayer is to begin to make our own journeys into the Scriptures of the Bible. Then we should perhaps read some great classics of the Christian faith. They can speak for us as we have never been able to do for ourselves, allowing us to know our own thoughts and feelings, perhaps even for the first time.

Another support to prayer is fasting. Fasting means to deprive ourselves of any activities or habits that are deeply ingrained into our lives. Stillness before God also encourages our growth in prayer. Gathering with friends to pray is an important activity.

Meet with a mentor—a more mature Christian—who is able to offer regular advice and direction in living the spiritual life. Spiritual direction is God-oriented, and its primary focus is on deepening and enriching a life of prayer. It helps us to move beyond seeing prayer as simply talking to God and presenting him with our needs to a more meditative and contemplative way of life, with prayer at its heart.

Our withdrawal into solitude, prayer, and meditation is also an affirmation of personal dependence on God to live in the world, rather than an escape from it. Withdrawal is necessary for us to listen to God, but true prayer must also relate to the needs of others and send us back into our relationships with new life.

We must make the connection between prayer and life. The closer you are to the heart of God, the closer you come to the heart of the world, and the closer you come to others.

We cannot comprehend all that God has planned for our lives. How can we get on with our lives when we are stunned and imprisoned in our own pain?

Think about Anna and what she was able to bring to others through her journey. The Gospel of Luke describes Anna as being "of a great age, having lived with her husband seven years after her marriage, then as a widow to the age of eighty-four. She never left the temple but worshipped there with fasting and prayer night and day" (Luke 2:36–37). Think of it: Anna, the aged woman, and Mary, the very young woman, meeting at such a crucial time. How much Mary must have needed her. Anna's early widowhood had given her a fuller understanding of life. She knew what suffering was. She had deepened her relationship with God over many years in the temple. She knew what surrender and fidelity meant. Anna came as a sign of hope and a source of strength for Mary. She came as a comfort to this young mother, who had just learned that she would have much sorrow in the future.

Our Annas come when we need them. Isn't that comforting? They come "just at the right time" in the form of a phone call, a letter, a person at the door, or a compassionate nurse at a bedside. They may not say a lot to us—they may not even realize how profoundly they are messengers of hope to us—but we know, and we gain courage from their presence. They bring us a touch of comfort and hope as we embark upon a time of suffering. Our Annas are messengers from God. They are compassion-filled people who are not afraid to be with someone who is hurting. They are faith-filled people who bring us encouragement as much by their presence as through their words. They are hope-filled people who bless us by their constant certainty of our ability to overcome adversity.

Sometimes our Annas have no idea that they are helping us with the pain that follows a Simeon announcement. Who is or was your Anna? Are you an Anna to someone in pain?

If you have experienced the loss of a loved one, whether it is a child, a spouse, a friend, or another family member, you probably have been given books on how to deal with your own grief by recognizing the steps of the grieving process.

I am not sure that I experienced each of the steps, or the order in which they are generally listed, but I do know from experience that holding tightly to our grief may make us become forgetful and unable to make decisions. Perhaps you were very organized before tragedy struck but now feel completely disorganized. Is that a sign of losing your mind? Not at all: it is a sign that you are going through the grieving process, and it is different for each individual. Suddenly, the easiest of tasks that we have always known become very difficult. We can get lost driving home from the store on the corner when we have shopped there for years. We might forget the ends of sentences or be unable to remember words or names. Sometimes we do not care how we look, how we feel, or what we do. We just feel sad, alone, and isolated.

We find ourselves crying over everything. Our eyes fill with tears when we least expect them, and they make trails down our cheeks. We become afraid to go places or see people, for fear that these unpredictable tears will begin to flow again. We also cry in a manner like none we have ever experienced before. It is a deep, wretched sobbing that we never imagine existed that comes from the bottoms of our stomachs.

Basically, the whole world seems to be turned upside down. A soft-spoken person may suddenly begin to act irrationally. Or someone who has always been outgoing is suddenly fearful of attending meetings or even leaving the house. We are pulled in opposite directions. We are agitated but too tired to move; we are lonely but do not want to be with others; we feel unloved, unloving, and unlovable, yet we need love desperately. We feel as if we have been abandoned with raw nerve endings.

Not only are we confused, lonely, and just not ourselves, but physical symptoms begin to hit without warning. We may experience hot flashes, cold sweats, insomnia, loss of appetite, tightness in the chest, panic about everything, or rapid breathing, and all of these things can be very distressing.

Many grieving persons ignore the danger signs, assuming that the discomfort is merely part of their grief. Often their lack of energy prevents them from seeking medical care. Some of the most minor ailments can become debilitating if they go untreated too long.

A survivor who has been involved in caring for her husband during a lengthy illness may have neglected her own health care during that time. And we are faced with the idea that we must be going crazy.

All of these things that I have mentioned are symptoms that are unexplained and never talked about: they are misunderstood feelings of profound grief. If you have experienced any of these feelings, consider going to have a check-up. Explain to your doctor what is going on in your life.

How long are we to remain grieving? When we are feeling such pain and anguish, we want to know when we will begin to feel better. We are accustomed to being on a schedule. Unfortunately, there is not a time chart that will answer the question of how long it will last. It takes time. It cannot be rushed, nor can it be gauged by anyone else's progress. The circumstances of the death can make a big difference in the grief period, as can the support systems the grieving person has available.

In June Cerza Kolf's book, *When Will I Stop Hurting?: Dealing with a Recent Death,* she states that there are four tasks that have been proven to aid in the grief process:

1. Facing the reality of the loss (letting go)

2. Experiencing the pain of grief (crying and talking about it)

3. Adjusting to the altered environment (acceptance)

4. Reinvesting emotional energy elsewhere (reaching out to others)

Often letting go of the grief becomes confused with letting go of our husband. We sometimes fear that if we let go of the group, then we will have nothing at all from the experience we have shared. Letting go does not mean to let go of the happy memories or to dispose of every single item the person owned. It means to be reasonable. It is reasonable to display photographs, to keep special belongings, and even to wear our husband's clothes—just not every minute of the day.

Healing can begin as the legalities are taken care of. Names may need to be changed on deeds or bank accounts. Legal documents need to be brought up to date. As we clean closets, sorting through the personal items to be saved or given away, we are aiding in the grief process.

In the book, *When the Crying's Done: A Journey Through Widowhood,* by Jeannette Kupfermann, she states on the inside cover: "Widows constitute a league of largely invisible women in our society. They are represented in the popular mind as 'merry,' 'rich,' 'lascivious,' but the reality is generally very different and the subject of widowhood is still surrounded by taboos and reticence which prevent the complex issues and problems from being confronted in an honest and frank way."

How true that statement is. We do become a league of our own with so much misunderstanding of our journeys—not only by ourselves but by others as well. This is why it is so important for communities to recognize these needs and to adopt a ministry, so widows may come together, work through their issues, find encouragement, and know they are not alone on their journeys. God has not forsaken us. He allowed these losses to happen in order to draw us closer to him and to serve him in ways we cannot imagine.

Widow2Widow and Brentwood Baptist Church hosted a widows' retreat in East Tennessee in September 2004. This was a wonderful time of fellowship and growth among these ladies, who came from all walks of life and from various states of the United States.

These ladies came together and bonded within the first evening. We enjoyed a time of laughter, some tears, and fellowship with others on the same journey.

One of the Bible studies we had was taught by Gayle Haywood, one of my Annas in my early journey of widowhood and the small groups minister at Brentwood Baptist Church in Brentwood, Tennessee. Gayle shared with us the plight of eagles and compared their grace, knowledge, and wisdom to what God has prepared us for and how we are meant to soar. I would like to share with you what I learned from Gayle about understanding the eagle and God's word.

Isaiah 40:31: "But they that wait upon the Lord shall renew their strength, they shall mount up with wings as eagles. They shall run, and not be weary, and they shall walk and not faint."

Did you know that an eagle knows when a storm is approaching long before it breaks? The eagle will fly to some high spot and wait for the winds to come.

When the storm hits, it sets its wings so that the wind will pick it up and lift it above the storm. While the storm rages below, the eagle is soaring above it. The eagle does not escape the storm. It simply uses the storm to lift it higher. It rises on the winds that bring the storm. When the storms of life come upon us—and all of us will experience them—we can rise above them by setting our minds and our belief toward God. The storms do not have to overcome us. We can allow God's power to lift us above them. God enables us to ride the winds of the storms that bring sickness, tragedy, failure, and disappointment into our lives. We can soar above the storms. Remember, it is not the burdens of life that weigh us down; it is how we handle them.

The Bible says, "Those who hope in the Lord will renew their strength. They will soar on wings like eagles" (Isaiah 40:31).

Psalm 102:5 says: "Who satisfieth thy mouth with good things; so that thy youth is renewed as the eagle's."

The eagle lives to a very great age. As he grows old, his beak becomes so long that he can no longer eat; then he flies away by himself to the top of a cliff and pecks on a rock until his bill falls off, after which a new bill grows in its place. While without the use of his bill, the bird also loses his feathers, because of fasting.

After the new bill grows and he again takes food, new feathers start growing so that he looks like a young eagle, going forth in a new covering with youthful beauty and strength. "Thy youth is renewed as the eagle's."

Deuteronomy 32:11 says: "As the eagle stirrith up her nest, fluttereth over her young, spreadeth abroad her wings, taketh them, beareth them on her wings."

Moses is telling the people how God deals with his children. The mother eagle watches her baby eaglets carefully. As they grow, she stirs them up a bit so they will not be contented to lie in the nest. She then flutters over them to make them want to use their wings as she does. Then she pushes them out of the nest and flies down beneath, carefully watching them so no harm will come to her children. When her mother's eye sees the little wings growing weary, she spreads out her great, strong wings, catches them, and bears them back to the nest for rest.

The nest is always very high. A fall would mean the end of flying, but the mother eagle knows when it is time to shake the young out of the nest and when to fly down to bring them back.

That is what God does for us: he bears us on eagle's wings.

Is it not a comforting thought to be compared to the wings of eagles?

My friend Peggy sometimes will travel with me when I speak, or she will even speak at some of my events when I feel led to have her be a part of them. Peggy has a song that she sings that is very fitting to our journey. Every time I hear her sing it, a peace completely absorbs me as I listen to her deliver the following words of the song. The song is entitled "He Is Able." Read these words and place yourself speaking them.

> Emotions run together in a flood of doubt and pain,
> We pray the best we can,
> But we must leave it in his hands
>
> Even though it seems to be impossible to me…
> He is able
>
> If he chooses not to move in the way we prayed he would…
> Be confident…He is working it all together for my good
>
> I will stand behind his Word, for he is able
>
> Questions seem to haunt us night and day.
> How could God allow our hearts to be torn this way?
> Does he listen when we call?
> Or is he even there at all?
>
> Yet I know when my eyes fail to see, he is able
> And even though it seems impossible to me, he is able
>
> But if he chooses not to move in the way we prayed he would…be confident
> he is working all together for our greater good
>
> I will stand behind his Word because he is able
> And as the night is in wait of dawning and if it ever fades away, I stand to face
> another day. I will stand behind his Word, for he is able

These words capture what God has placed on my heart in ministering and mentoring women of all walks of life—who are on their journeys or yet to be on the journey of widowhood.

Going back once again to the subject of grief, let's look at a few things that might be of help to you. People often think of grief as the result of the loss of a loved one. But grief can come from any significant loss. Anything a person loses that is near and dear to him or her will cause grief to some degree.

Grief is a normal part of life. It is a normal mechanism that God has given to help us deal with losses that occur in our lives. If grief is indeed natural and is a part of everyone's life, why is it seldom spoken of? Why is there discomfort when someone mentions the death of a loved one? Why is there embarrassment when tears come in the midst of an ordinary conversation? Grief is not something to be ashamed of or to be avoided.

In the *Grief Recovery Handbook* by James and Friedman, grief is normal, natural, and clearly the most powerful of all emotions. It is also the most neglected and misunderstood experience, often by the griever as well as those around them.

Grief is not an enemy or a sign of weakness. It is a sign of being human. Grief is the cost of loving someone or something of value.

Death is a part of life. Death is, of course, the most dramatic loss we anticipate and experience in life. We all lose people close to us through death. Our lives are marked by a variety of losses. Some are life-changing: leaving home, the death of a loved one, or divorce. Others are subtle: changing jobs, moving, or a broken friendship.

The loss of a close family member can create extra depth and complexity to your grief. Perhaps you shared a special and intimate connection with your loved one, and this relationship helped you define who you are. Losing this person has literally ripped you apart on the inside, leaving you unsure of your own identity.

Loss can threaten your identity, your self-esteem, and your hope for future happiness. There is hope. Your identity can be found again when you abide in the Lord Jesus Christ and place your faith in him.

One reason grief disrupts so many aspects of your life is that your loss is not one isolated loss. You will miss so many qualities and facets of the person you lost that each will become an opportunity to experience grief.

The reality of these losses needs to be acknowledged and incorporated into our understanding of ourselves and the world. This is what it means to recover from loss. The process we go through in this particular recovery journey is called grief.

Grief affects everything you do. It can disrupt every aspect of your life in ways you might not expect. Say your losses out loud to God; speak until you run out of words to say. He knows your deepest needs, and he alone can provide.

Unresolved grief will multiply your problems. Express your emotions, share your story, get angry if you need to, and tell God how you really feel. The person you lost would not want you to become trapped in a continual cycle of grief. It is not a betrayal of that person for you to get better. Getting better means you move away from the disabling aspects of grief. You don't stop missing them or feeling the hole left in your heart.

Your steps through the grieving process may be halting baby steps. As difficult as it may be, God wants you to walk forward through your grief. Grief does not just go away with time. It is not like a bad cold that you just have to "get over."

You don't get over grief; it is not something that we recover from. It is a process that helps us to recover from many losses we experience.

Grief helps you to get *through* your loss. It makes it possible for us to face the painful reality of our losses, incorporate those losses into understanding, and somehow move on.

The purpose of grief is *not* to forget what we have lost, but to help us grow in understanding, compassion, and courage in the midst of our losses. Grief is not an ending or a walking away from what we have lost. Forgetting the person or the dream that died is not the same as recovery from loss. Recovery from loss allows us to reshape our relationship with the person or the dream we have lost and to find ways to grow in our new circumstances.

> No one ever said life was fair or easy.
>
> This may be the most difficult time in your life.
>
> The confusion and hurt raise many questions. *Why* did this happen to me?
>
> *Why* do bad things happen to good people?
>
> There are no simple answers.
>
> God does not abandon us in crisis.

There are common feelings associated with grief, but God has made us all individuals with individual personalities, minds, and emotions. Not only that, but each loss is different. You have as much right to deal with your grief in your own way as another person does in theirs, as long as it isn't sinful or harmful to others.

No one else has the right to expect you to deal with it in her way. It is *your* grief, not theirs.

Grief does not simply go away when the funeral is over, when the bankruptcy has been filed, or when the divorce has been finalized. It does not go away at any certain time. Some think it should go away after the one-year anniversary of the loss, but that isn't always true. In fact, it may never fully go away. There may always be a "scar." But we do want to get to the point of accepting the loss as best we can.

You will need time to grieve. Each person's timetable for healing is different. All losses are not the same loss. All grief is not the same grief.

Grief is emotionally painful. It allows us to heal and to grow, but the cost in emotional energy is often very high. Because of this, we often seek ways to postpone the disciplines of grief.

Society wants us to get over it and move on with our lives. But in Ecclesiastes 3:3, God understands the process it will take to heal. God understands that even though we may have buried a loved one, we cannot bury our feelings. We need time to vent—and to invent ways of coping with the loss.

Because we are loving individuals, grief will visit our lives many times. Grief is a deep, intense mental suffering caused by loss. The pain of sorrow is an inevitable companion to the joy of living. It is part of the baggage of trials and tribulations that we must carry through this world…but *God promised his blessings in the midst of pain, and his presence in our darkest hour.*

As we endure grief and other adversities of life, his Word reminds us that our "light and momentary troubles are achieving for us an eternal glory that outweighs them all" (2 Corinthians 4:17).

Once you realize that grief is a natural, healthy, and self-corrective process that enables you to recover from a terrible emotional wound, you won't fall prey to the guilt that Christians sometimes feel when grieving for a lost loved one.

With a new prespective on grief, you will see it as God's instrument for healing a broken heart. Grief has the power to shake every part of our lives. It can alter our behavior, rattle our emotions, and scramble our thinking. Relationships can easily be rocked as we try to cope with fragile feelings and uncertain circumstances. Even our physical health can become impaired.

The days immediately following an unexpected loss are often very social times. Friends may reach out to one who has experienced loss for a week or two. The difficult times of loneliness usually come later, when the extreme pain of loss is beginning to yield to the longer-term pain of the recovery process.

Loneliness can be a very significant struggle during this time. People do not know what to say and often say foolish things.

In the book *Facing the Death of Someone You Love* by Elisabeth Elliot, she describes six simple things to help you through this valley, and, if done in faith, they can be the way to resurrection.

1. Try to be still and know that he is God (Psalm 46).

2. Try to give thanks. (Thank God for the promise of his presence.)

3. Refuse self-pity: it is a death that has no resurrection.

4. Accept the loneliness. (When God takes a loved person from your life, it is in order to call you, in a new way, to himself.)

5. Offer your loneliness up to God.

6. Do something for somebody else.

Isaiah 58:10–12 says: "If you pour yourself out for the hungry and satisfy the desire of the afflicted, then you shall rise in the darkness and your gloom be as the noonday. And the Lord will guide you continually and satisfy your desire with good things, and make your bones strong; and you shall be like a watered garden, like a spring of water, whose waters fail not, and…you shall be called a repairer of the breach, the restorer of the streets to dwell in." (Or, in another translation, a restorer of "the paths leading home.")

Turn your energies toward satisfaction, not of your own needs, but of those of others. People who are doing the emotionally painful work of grief need friends who will follow the Scripture: "Mourn with those who mourn." They need to re-experience the comforting presence of Jesus, who is a "man of sorrows, acquainted with grief."

Most of us find it difficult to give ourselves permission to grieve. We are disappointed that it takes so long to adapt to losses. We are distressed that the emotions involved are so painful. We feel we should be able to handle it better. We wonder if something is wrong with us. And yes, we even wonder about God. Is God disappointed in our grief? It may come as a shock to those of us who have trouble grieving to learn that God grieves as well.

Sometimes our losses seem to go unnoticed. We may minimize the reality of the losses we experience. We may also deny that losses have an emotional impact on us. Or maybe we are aware of our loss and the emotional pain that comes with it, but others have not noticed. Other people may down play the significance of our loss, or discount the pain we feel.

For grief to lead to healing and spiritual growth, our losses need to be identified and acknowledged. We need to pay attention to the losses we have experienced, and we need others to pay attention as well. The Bible teaches us that God pays attention to our losses. He does not minimize them or deny their reality.

In Ro Sunderland's book, *Getting Through Grief,* he lists some things he calls "the work of mourning":

1. **Accepting the reality of loss.** William Worden emphasized the importance of this task, noting that when someone dies, there is always a sense that it has not happened. Accepting the pain and readjusting to the

environment marks the final abandonment of the dream to somehow recapture the deceased. It means, for widows, undertaking tasks like balancing a checkbook, making business decisions without the consultation of a spouse, or remembering the children will not graduate with their peers or grow up so that the parent and child may relate as adults, friends, and confidants.

2. **Working through painful feelings.** Feelings of shock, numbness, and disbelief are characteristic of the early period of bereavement, often accompanied by feelings of intense anxiety, evoked by the mourner's fear of "going crazy." *Bereaved* stems from the Old German root *berauben,* passing into Old English as the verb "to be reaved"—meaning "robbed." With this context, if directed at God, feelings of anger can lead to guilt, which may further intensify and prolong grief.

3. **Struggling back from depression.**

4. **Deciding to take up one's life again, to treasure memories.** One of the most demanding challenges of grief involves reinvesting in life. New relationships and new dreams are offered to us. New joy is possible. That which is new, however, may feel uncomfortable. We may feel it is somehow wrong to experience the joys of life again. We will be acutely aware that any time we open ourselves to new love or to new hope; we also open ourselves to the possibility of new loss.

People may try to find meaning in our loss long before we have prepared for the thought ourselves. Although grief can leave us feeling very alone, it is the consistent testimony of the Bible that God reaches out to us in times when we are alone. God does not abandon his people who struggle with loneliness as part of their recovery from loss.

Grief is a cup of sorrow: though it is bitter, you must drink the entire cup and let your grief run its natural course. Put your faith in all of God's promises and assurances. You must trust that your God and loving Heavenly Father knows best and that his understanding is perfect. God's desire to give comfort knows no boundaries. We must reach out and accept it.

Through prayer and meditation in the Word, find a place in God's presence where he can shower you with his love and wrap his arms around you—as a loving Father would his hurting child.

Spend time reading the Bible, and allow the Holy Spirit to minister to your wounded heart with the healing of God's eternal word.

Dinah Maria Mulock Craik has said that during a time of loss and suffering, a special form of grace can rest on you. It is unexplainable in human terms, but with it you acquire a supernatural peace that transcends your circumstances.

To access this grace, pause where you are and begin to pour out your heart to God. Exchange your present feelings for his tranquility. Nothing you can say will offend God; he has heard it all. Nothing that you think will disturb him. Just speak to him like a cherished friend, and ask for a generous dose of peace that passes all understanding.

As you lay your heart before God, expect to receive the unlimited resources of his kingdom. Take all you need.

God's passion sits stored and waiting to be measured out at a moment's notice to anyone who asks. God is your refuge, a tower of strength in your day of trouble, so run to him. Give him your confusion, and let him comfort you as his child.

Christ came to heal the brokenhearted. It gives him joy to lift your spirit of heaviness with his healing oil of gladness. Ask him for the kind grace that will enable you to stand firm when all your strength is gone. He gives freely and generously to all who ask for his help. Position your heart to run toward the path of God's presence. Picture yourself seated with Christ in heavenly places each time the cares of your life overwhelm you. When you are tempted to take the weight of your heartache onto your own shoulders, make yourself pray. Day and night, keep up a running conversation with the grace-giver. Hour by hour, give him your hurt, fears, and loneliness.

With God comes a river of perfect peace that runs near your heart twenty-four hours a day. Reach for it. Let it trickle down the cracks and soak dry places in your soul. Through every season of the soul, may God's grace and peace be yours in abundance.

Our times of sorrow equip us to minister to others when they are hurting. God expects us to learn something from every circumstance in our lives, including grief.

As Christians, our purpose in life is to become more like Jesus. That means reaching out to others with compassion and comfort in their time of need and using our experiences and understanding to help them cope.

Before you speak to a grieving friend, pray and ask God for guidance about when to speak and what to say. Encourage the griever to talk about her feelings. Encourage her to seek refuge in the God of all comfort.

Be a good listener and don't judge what is said. The best thing you can do to help is to listen with compassion. They need true friends that will listen not only with their ears but with their hearts.

Don't push. Let the griever guide the discussion on their grief.

Pray for the griever and offer scriptures, without preaching, when she indicates openness.

Share these points about grieving: it is natural and healthy; it can be a source of blessing from God; it is not a sin.

Never tell a grieving person that it is God's will, but do say that your love and prayers are with them.

How to Grieve:

Be good to yourself…grieving is a tough job.

Feel the feelings…emotions are normal and healthy.
Get angry…direct your anger in healthy ways.

Listen to yourself…you will know what you need.

Set limits…don't be afraid to say *no* to yourself or to others.

Stay active…part of taking care of yourself is going on.

Cry…it is okay…tears are only liquid emotions.

Your faith…find comfort in the word and God's promises.

Read about grief…so you will know that you are normal.

Ask for support…give someone a gift by letting her be there for you.

We cannot always understand the "why," but we can lay hold of the "who." No matter what happens to us, no matter what the loss, God's hand is still offered to us.

The Bible affirms the need to grieve and express sorrow. Perhaps the only way to get through grief is to let Christ wrap his pierced hands around your broken heart and allow him to share in your sufferings.

In Psalm 56, a list of tears is mentioned. Think of all the tears you've cried. You may have thought no one noticed your red eyes, but God sees. He has every intention of rewarding your endurance of that pain. Why would he meticulously chronicle every one of your tears? Every tear will be redeemed. God will give you indescribable glory for your grief, not with a general wave of the hand, but in a considered and specific way. Each tear has been listed; each will be recompensed. Just think, when you finally get to heaven, you won't have to dry your own tears. According to Revelations 21:4, he will wipe away every tear from our eyes.

The book of Jeremiah demonstrates that God gives strong hope even to those who can't stop weeping. And it proves that while some of us are ordained in the providence of God to a lifetime of hardship and tears, we can endure by clinging to the hope God offers.

Micca Campbell (excerpt from the NIV Encouragement Bible) explained grief and joy in the following way:

> While some grief, such as death, may take a lifetime to heal, the good news is that during that lifetime you can, once again, experience joy. Over the years, I've found joy by discovering that my grief is in fact working for my good.
>
> Still, having joy doesn't mean that I will never feel pain. God created my emotions, so it's acceptable to grieve. On the other hand, I don't have to remain in dismay. Looking at my life before grief, during grief and after grief; combined with God's Word, I began to see the purpose of my burden. God was at work in my grief, making me perfect, complete and lacking in nothing.
>
> My life during grief was lonely without him. I felt angry and betrayed by the God I had loved since I was a little child. I locked those feelings in my heart, as if God didn't know how I felt toward Him. Then one night I reached a desperate point and cried out to God. Bursting through the door to the throne room of grace, I shook my fist in His face and boldly questioned, "Why—why did you do this to me? Oh God, I need to know why!" Just as a mother runs to her screaming child, so did God the Father run to me, His child. I didn't see Him with my eyes or touch Him with my hands, but I felt His presence consume me as if God poured Himself over my entire body. In the comfort of His presence, I was compelled to read Psalm 139: "Is there any place you can go from my spirit? If you climb to the sky, I am there! If you go underground, I am there!" I knew then that my Lord had not betrayed me. He had come to say "I am Here!"
>
> Healing began as I cried out to God and allowed Him to carry me through the painful moments. This process continued until He lifted me to a new level of grace. Life after death grew bright, as I focused on His promises instead of my circumstances. Grief usually offers two choices. I can despise it and die in my anger and bitterness or I can live again by confessing my feelings and trusting God. I chose life.
>
> Consequently, grief has made me stronger, more mature and patient so that I'm able to handle trials to come. Plus, I've learned that joy can be found by believing that God loves me in all things and is working for my good, conforming me to the image of Christ. God also has kept His promises.

How can you experience joy in the midst of your grief? First, draw close to God by crying out and allowing Him to meet you in your pain. Second, stop asking "What am I going to do?" Instead, ask "What is God going to do?" God is not working to destroy you, but to recreate you. He is making you strong and Christ-like so that you're able to finish the race. Finally, choose life by trusting God and not your circumstances. As you do, you'll gain a renewed love for Him, as His love enables you to encompass joy in the midst of your grief.

We are constantly on the move, particularly when we have suddenly lost a husband to death. We think that if we stay busy enough and fill our schedules, we can avoid the pain and suffering. We are stretched beyond our maximum capacity by the demands of our lives. We are torn between what must be done and what we should do, but trying to put it all into action sometimes is not possible in today's hectic society.

We know we need to stop and seek opportunities to rest, plan, and regroup, as well as to draw closer to God. The truth is that the door to stillness is waiting for us to open it and go through, but it will not open by itself. We need to choose to make stillness a part of our lives.

If we are to live wisely, we must learn to balance the time we spend in quiet and calm with the time we spend in the fray of everyday life. Ecclesiastes 3:1 says, "There is a time for everything." This includes a time and place to cultivate stillness in the midst of your busy, productive life.

It is imperative for us to get away from everything and everybody on a regular basis for thought, prayer, and rest. Stillness is the key to keeping ourselves from becoming frazzled and out of control. It is as necessary as it is to sleep, exercise, and eat nutritious food. Perspective is lost when these are out of balance.

People who make time for stillness are the people who have the energy and perspective to stay on top of their hectic lives. As we seek God for direction, he will open the door to discovering ways to implement our needed quiet times.

An appointment on a calendar is a commitment most of us are able to keep. Stillness can be captured in short moments of solitude. Write out Scripture verses on index cards, and meditate on them while doing the dishes. I sometimes put sticky notes on my computer to remind me of what I need to do, or to have a special notation for prayer. I have also been known to put sticky-note prayers on my vanity, so when I am putting on my makeup in the mornings or brushing my teeth at night before going to bed, I will have a reminder. I have even posted them on the dashboard of my car to reach those moments in traffic or on long stretches of highway. Keep a Bible in the car, leave early for an appointment, and spend a few moments with the Lord. Try turning off the radio and praying while you travel.

There are things that can only be accomplished as we meet with the Lord in quiet time. It is in our quiet moments that we get a handle on so many challenging aspects of our lives.

Retreating to a quiet place helps us to discover stillness. To people who are overstimulated and worn down by the constant barrage of life, the spirit of stillness and time alone with God are lifesavers.

Stay in tune with God. God's Word is the foundation of my security and strength. It is through daily Scripture reading, prayer, and meditation that I can tap into God's strength and love and get a handle on what he wants for my life. My friend Kitty, who happens to be another one of my Annas, has taught me so much in the grace God has extended to her, and it is because she searches and makes time to spend in God's Word and to meditate on a daily basis.

Sometimes I cannot meditate, so I will begin to read a devotional or a prayer. I will write out prayers in a journal. When there is an answer to a prayer, I am sure to make a notation—to praise God with a thankful heart for his love and guidance. When we look back at what we have written, it also serves as evidence of our spiritual growth, which is a result of growing faith. This is the one thing I would want my loved ones to find after I am gone, as evidence of my faith. Our obedience is strengthened as we write out the promises God gives us. At times during your Scripture reading, a certain verse will hold special meaning for you. Take a moment and write it down, as this is a way God communicates his promises to us. You will also discover that if you write it down, the verse can encourage you each time you reflect on your writing.

When God brings someone to mind, take a moment in prayer and write an encouraging note to assure her of God's love and to let her know of your prayers.

Spiritual growth takes place as we listen to God's Word through Scripture, prayer, and fellow believers, and then act in obedience to that word. One-on-one times with God are essential to your growth, but alone they are not enough. To grow we need to share love, support, and prayers with others.

God is our shepherd, and he will guide us as we seek him. He will provide every resource we need in order to walk with him. If you plan ahead and make time for those things you truly value, including times of stillness, you can be sure that God's strength will carry you through the many demands you find on your life.

For those of you who have never been on this journey, I am going to try to educate you about a few situations that I have experienced, with the help of "On Mission" articles from the Women's Missionary Union (WMU).

The trauma of losing a spouse to death is one of the most devastating events in the life of any person. Expressing Christ-like, unconditional love toward a widow will help her as she struggles to begin a frightening new life alone. This is a time when nonbelievers may be open to the gospel, as they contemplate the eternal destiny of their husbands and their own final destinations.

A widow wants to hear her husband's name, to feel the comfort of his presence through words. Encourage her to share her feelings, but do not force her to do so. If she wants to talk, listen attentively, and then prayerfully comment. Simple answers such as, "I can only guess how deeply you hurt," or "I am so glad you are talking to me," are comforting and nonintrusive.

When a widow alludes to painful memories, avoid statements about the good health your family or friends are experiencing. Such comments are hurtful because she senses you have not grasped the pain she is feeling. It may even add to her grief, making her feel that God doesn't love her as much as he loves others, or he would have healed her husband too.

By spending time with a widow and explaining that you are doing so because the Bible instructs us to look after widows, Christians can lead a nonbeliever to understand that she is important to God and that he loves her. Give her confidence so she will put her faith in him.

Widows who experience feelings of insecurity may withdraw. Assure her that God loves her and that she is special to him. Explain that his choice is not to protect her from grief but to give her strength and peace to deal with her loss. As you minister to a nonbeliever, she will see your sincerity and trust you. Then you can explain that Christ wants her to trust him.

A grieving widow is trying to come to terms with losing her husband and facing life without him. Remarks, such as, "It's time to get over it," can inflict sorrow because the widow knows she cannot throw away those years she and her husband spent loving each other.

Be sensitive to a widow's mood. Many times, a smile cannot radiate through her painful memories. Your words assuring her of God's promises to take care of her can become a beacon for her, a reflection of him in you. This way, you are serving God and showing the non-Christian widow that Christ sees and hears her pain.

Avoid telling the widow that God healed someone else because of his or her faith and prayers. Often, the widow is already dealing with inner conflict about why God did not heal her husband after her fervent prayers. This is the hope of all believers. God is a loving God, and it is his will for all to believe and be healed in heaven.

If you have never lost a spouse, it is better not to say that you understand. The widow's pain is too deep—the sorrows too overwhelming for you to pretend you understand how she feels, because she didn't feel that way until her husband died.

At home, at church, or wherever you meet a widow, words such as, "I still miss seeing your husband," bond the widow with you; they show that her husband meant something to you and has not been forgotten. If appropriate, say something like, "He was a good man and loved the Lord," "He had a wonderful sense of humor," or "I remember when…" Say whatever is appropriate, but be sincere. A widow who hears your memories of her husband will embrace your friendship.

Share a personal experience of loss with the nonbelieving widow. By doing so, you will help her understand that Jesus strengthened you during a difficult time. As a non-Christian sees Christ in you, encourage her to seek God's eternal love through the gift of his Son.

Give the widow a chance to enjoy her husband's memory with you. If she cries, that is okay! She will remember you with fondness for letting her remember him. It is not necessary to dwell on the husband, but let the widow know you have not forgotten him and that he had a valuable place during his life.

A widow's hurt is deeply ingrained, and she is facing a new lifestyle alone. If you knew the couple before the husband died, don't stop calling his widow. She is already coping with feelings of low self-worth, feelings that she is no longer a whole person. Let her know that you remember her, and that you care for her as much as you did before her husband died.

A card with a verse such as Psalm 116:15, "Precious is the sight of the Lord is the death of his saints," comforts the widow. It reminds her that God loved her husband and wanted him to be with him for some special purpose.

A Christian can send a note of encouragement or a poem sharing God's love and his promises for us and our loved ones. These are tangible messages that will be reread many times.

11

Building a Ministry of Compassion and Comfort

I am going to share with you how to build a ministry of compassion and comfort.

The mission of Widow2Widow is to offer encouragement, comfort, support, and guidance to women who are dealing with the loss of their husbands. Each group that forms and uses the name Widow2Widow must cohere to this mission statement, but they are individual groups with no ties to the organization itself.

Widow2Widow is a 501(c)(3) nonprofit organization with the goal to minister to the needs of widows and to assist churches and communities in helping widows of all ages, races, and religious backgrounds to overcome problems in their life's journeys.

The overall organization provides support to widows through organized local Widow2Widow support groups that help widows to understand and cope with the problems and concerns they may experience in their daily lives. The organization also provides a curriculum to any church or organization interested in establishing a Widow2Widow ministry. Widow2Widow holds inspirational seminars, workshops, retreats, and conferences for widows and those who are leading ministries to help others on this journey.

Widow2Widow offers inspirational materials and guides to help widows to adjust to the changes in their lives and to continue on their journeys as women of God. We help train deacons, elders, and church staff in the needs of widows and how to respond appropriately.

This ministry is needed in our communities to help minister to the hearts and spiritual growth of widows and to encourage them to find homes in God through his Word and other believers. This is an ongoing mission to care and to love these ladies on their journeys into and through widowhood, as we hold true to the command of James 1:27 "to care for the orphans and widows."

Because Widow2Widow is open to widows of all ages, we have formed another organization under the incorporation called Young Widow2Widow. This ministry is designed specifically for young widows on their journeys, who possibly have minor children still at home. The needs of young widows vary greatly, because they have been robbed of their futures in growing old with their husbands and were most likely left as single moms in the process.

Regardless of which ministry you may be considering for your church, your family member, or your friend, the first step is to pray about what God would have you do. Read the Scripture 2 Corinthians 1:3–4: "Praise be to the God and Father of our Lord Jesus Christ, the Father of compassion and the God of all comfort, who comforts us in all our troubles, so that we can comfort those in any trouble with the comfort we ourselves have received from God."

Again, the first step in starting a widows' ministry is to pray. Pray for what God would have you and your church or community do. Pray for the ladies who will be involved in having organizational roles and for those that are on their journeys and need comforting—as well as those yet to be on the journey.

Find a facilitator and a co-leader for your group. It is more beneficial if they are widows who have experienced or are in the process of experiencing the journey. God already has these ladies picked out, and he is waiting for your prayers and commitments. He will reveal all you need and equip you with everything imaginable.

When I began this ministry, I was blind to all that was before me, and it was a true step of faith in God. I had never done anything like this, and the main question I asked myself was: *What could anyone learn from me?* What did I have to offer? What is the answer? I don't have anything to offer on my own. I can only offer what the Holy Spirit has graced me with to touch so many lives.

I cannot express to you how blessed my life is to be on the journey of widowhood under very trying circumstances—and yet to have God place widows in my path to love and comfort. It has helped me in a tremendous way to get through my own grief by helping others.

Through our experiences and the suffering we have witnessed in the lives of others, we have learned that we need one another.

Most of us, though, are uncomfortable about asking for help and exposing our needs. Have you thought that, through living through your husband's illness or the sudden news of his death, there was something God wanted to teach you and your family? Are you meant to learn to trust in him to meet your every need? Does he want to teach the local body of Christ the true meaning of serving him? Think about this: even through those tough moments when we did not feel we would be able to take another breath, we were being blessed in the smallest of ways. The cards, meals, phone calls, prayers: all of that is what others were giving to us. God's people were being blessed because they were learning to give, to sacrifice, and to put their faith in action. Not asking for help and not sharing the needs of your family or yourself is robbing the local body of Christ of a blessing.

Talk to the leadership of your church about what you would like to do for widows. Explain how we are commanded repeatedly in the Bible to care for widows, yet many churches have left this up to individuals. Explain that there is a curriculum and a ministry that is quickly growing because it belongs to God. Spread the word within your church about the needs of widows and what can be done about them.

Go to the church secretary and obtain a list of widows in your congregation—or go to the local funeral homes and talk to them about this ministry; perhaps they might help to sponsor. This is where you can get your initial list of addresses to begin to communicate with other widows and get them involved.

Write a letter of introduction, explaining that you are led to begin this ministry, and have a profile for each lady to complete. Ask them if they know of someone that might be interested, or who has a need to be a part of fellowship and encouragement. Include the idea and the vision you have for this ministry.

Decide when you want to have your first meeting. Generally, you can meet once a month or more often. The meetings generally last about two hours if they are monthly meetings. Because this involves Christian women, there are usually refreshments involved!

After your first meeting, you might find out what the needs are and ask the ladies what topics would be beneficial for them to explore. Find speakers (you can usually find someone within your church that is qualified at no cost), and see if they are available for any of the dates you have worked out for your meetings. Treat this as if you are having a fellowship time together with your Sunday school class. It is that simple.

Send the ladies cards, and help them to understand that this ministry is not a time to gather and feel sorry for themselves and relive their experiences. That may come at some point, but the idea of the ministry is to offer a time of encouragement. We have enough sorrow every day; we need to know that when we arrive, we are going to be truly blessed.

Let me share with you a few ideas from experience. By trade, I was an accountant until I got involved in ministry. I am not creative, and I am very straightforward. But, in spite of all of that, I do have a sense of humor.

One Thanksgiving, I wanted the ladies to feel very special. I wanted this meeting to be something they would remember when Thanksgiving Day arrived, particularly if it was their first holiday without their husbands.

I mailed invitations (as I usually do), and the only hint on the invitation of what I had in store was the invitation's design itself. The invitation was a luau shirt, and it told of a luncheon for the ladies on the Saturday before Thanksgiving.

I decorated the parlor of my church in nothing but beach and luau stuff. The tables had grass skirts and shells all over them. I had palm trees and beach balls everywhere. I was dressed in a grass skirt, a beachcomber hat, and a coconut bra. Yes, you read correctly: a coconut bra. Let me say this: coconuts are not shaped like we are! Thank goodness I wore a shirt underneath my coconuts.

The ladies arrived, and they were greeted with hugs. (Always greet with a hug—it does wonders!) After the hug, they were given a flower lei. Their nametags had their regular names and their Hawaiian names, which I looked up in advance on the Internet. The Internet and the Oriental Trading Company can do wonders for your theme parties.

I had Hawaiian music playing in the background, and we just had the best time. I had Tommye dressed up in a grass skirt with her cane; we even did the hula together. The church has never been the same!

I provided lunch for the ladies, which was catered by a member of the church who had experience in theme parties. I also had a small budget with the church to help pay for all of this because I didn't want to charge the ladies anything.

We played games, and I had door prizes that had been donated.

I had never heard as much laughter as there was in that room. My coconuts kept sliding all around, and I got tired of them, so I turned them into serving platters and served the ladies nuts and mints. The older ladies gave me a hard time during all of the laughter and said that that is what happens when you get older: your breasts sag and you need something to truly hold them up and support them.

I wanted this to be something that would help them through the holiday if necessary. On Thanksgiving Day, I received a hysterical phone call from one of the ladies who had been at our luau. I thought she was crying, and I knew it was her first holiday without her husband. Once she calmed down, she told me how the family had enjoyed their meal together and gave thanks for the ministry, because her daughter-in-law had put a coconut bowl on the table filled with nuts, and the widow had begun to laugh. Her family thought she had truly lost it until she told them about the experience she'd had at the meeting the Saturday before.

This is what the ministry is about. We have fun.

Another theme meeting (again at Thanksgiving, the next year) was a Mardi Gras party. When the ladies arrived, they were greeted with their hugs and then given masks and beads to hang around their necks. Our guest speaker was a widow and had written a book, but she was also from New Orleans, and she told us about the original Mardi Gras with the costumes and the beads and the balls. She told us about King Cake, and she even shared her experience of being a widow. We played games, and again, the women gave themselves permission to laugh and realize that happiness was just as healing as the releasing of tears.

We have had tea parties, craft parties, and just a lot of fun in fellowship with others who are on this journey.

One of the walls that I come up against is the widows who have been widowed a very long time and do not feel they need such a group. They could be of such help by mentoring other widows new to the journey. There is so much potential in meeting the needs of widows.

This ministry helps by offering God's promises to the ladies. God doesn't promise us a life of mountaintop experiences. There will be valleys to go through. There will be dark valleys. There will be disorienting valleys. The valleys of depression and despair are real. What he promises is not a road map that will give us a detour around those valleys, but that he will walk through those valleys with us.

When we emerge from those experiences, we look back and realize that it is where the growth is. It isn't on the mountaintops, above the timberline; it is in the valleys.

We all suffer in our own ways. God made us to be individuals, and we react differently to different circumstances. We are not to judge how people suffer; we are to love them through it. There is really no proper way to suffer. Suffering is not tidy. Suffering is a purifying process, a process of cleaning out impurities. When suffering causes impurities to rise to the surface, we are going to see the worst of people. Their selfishness is going to come out, their bad priorities are going to become apparent, and they are not going to be able to mask their sinfulness anymore. Suffering breaks down the walls that people put up to hide what's really inside.

Joni Eareckson Tada says it best: "By itself, suffering does no good. But when we see it as the thing between God and us, it has meaning. Wedged in the cross, suffering becomes a transaction. The cross is the place of transaction. The cross is the power of God. It is the place where power happens between God and us."

When we minister to one another, sometimes the words aren't there for us to tell them how much we want to help, because really we wish we could take the pain away. I know that I wished someone would take the pain away for me. But then there are those who mean well—who have not a clue about what I am experiencing—because they haven't gone through that journey.

Here are some words that might be of help in honoring pain:

- I cannot begin to understand the pain you are feeling, but I'm here to be with you.
- I know I can't make your pain go away, but I want to help.
- Would you like to talk?
- Can I give you a hug?
- Tell me how you really feel. I want to know.
- I can see that you are hurting; do you want someone to cry with?
- Do you want to be alone, or would you like a friend nearby?

What we must understand is that God hates suffering. Jesus spent much of his life relieving it. He specifically says that all who follow him can expect hardship. Do we really think we should be exempt from suffering? Hebrews 5:8 tell us that we cannot be greater than our Master. If he has suffered, we must expect to suffer as well. Jesus considers our sufferings to be his sufferings. He feels the sting in his chest when we hurt. He takes it personally. This is intimacy described from Jesus' perspective.

Widow2Widow offers encouraging ideas by motivating ordinary people to do extraordinary things. Everyone needs frequent words of encouragement.

In Romans and Acts, Scripture mentions mourning with those who mourn. This is the widow ministry in a nutshell. I have learned to stand beside widows, cry with them, hold their hands, and just be present. I have learned that those who mourn will be comforted, so I let them mourn. I even encourage it. I understand that mourning is a necessary part of dealing with loss. It is not a weakness in faith.

God commands us to show our grief in Romans 12:15. I know that I am not capable of relieving the pain, but I also know there's no way to get around the pain either. We must go through it before we can get to the other side of it and grow in our spiritual walk and perhaps even help others in the process.

I am amazed at what God had to take me through to change me from avoiding suffering people to comforting those who are in pain and distress. He had to take me through a tremendous amount of pain to prepare me for this ministry of comfort. He had to change my heart. I don't know exactly how He did it or when He did it, but I can tell you where He did it. It was in the valley of my own suffering. I didn't orchestrate any of this; I didn't even welcome it at the time. I have known the fellowship of suffering, and I have joined the ranks of all those who became useful to God through the things that they suffered. Praise God!

12

Conclusion

My journey through widowhood has not been easy, but I don't believe it is an easy journey to bear. I don't know how widows go through this life-altering path without God, not believing in his divine promises and not feeling his loving arms surrounding them.

As I recall the time of losing my son and giving up on my faith all of those years ago, I don't know how we managed to be so angry at God. We serve an awesome God that will always love us through our pain, even if we cannot feel his presence at the time. He is there, waiting for us to recognize him and blessing us with the love that only he can provide. His comfort cannot be measured. He is forever faithful, even though we may become angry and pull away.

I wish there were things in my life that I would have done differently, such as my walk with God in those earlier years. But God knew what it was going to take in order for me to come back to him. He knew when I married Stan that I would only have a life with him for a few years but that my life with God would be eternal. God knew it was going to take Stan's untimely death to bring me back to him, and it had to follow the path orchestrated as it was. If Stan had died in my arms, would I have made the same choices? If Stan had died while driving with our son, would I have Tyler today, for God to use him in my walk and the walks of many others?

In order for me to follow what God would lead me to do, everything had to happen as it did. I had to wander in the world for all of my young adult life so that the purpose would be fulfilled in my middle age. Yes, I am wiser now. Would I rather have Stan back than to experience all of these things that God has blessed me with? I can't really answer that. I like who I have become in my walk with God; I like to be referred to as a woman of God. I still miss Stan very much, but as much as I loved him in life, it was his death that has served God in many ways. I have had the honor of comforting and ministering to thousands of women.

I asked my son recently if, by chance, anything were to happen to me right now, what words he would use to describe his mother. His words were something like, "She loves and cares for many. Her smile can calm most people and make them feel comforted. She allows others to be the way they need to be and loves them through it."

What would your family and friends say about you? What legacy will you leave behind? Have you ever thought of those things?

I know that when Stan died I found things in his belongings that were not pleasing to God or to me. I have learned so much from his passing, and I do know where he is, and I look forward to the time I will be reunited with all of those that I loved who have preceded me in death.

My life with Stan was filled with love and happiness. But his death has brought me closer to God, and it has brought me a relationship with my son that might not have happened otherwise. Do I still miss Stan? Oh, praise God, yes. Every day. But because I had a wonderful first marriage, even with its problems, I have an even more wonderful second marriage to Larry, who in his own way has taught me many things that I would not have learned otherwise.

As Tyler mentioned, when Larry came into our family, Stan was in heaven, standing next to Jesus, helping pick out a new man to fulfill the roles in our lives that he no longer could. That is the kind of husband and father Stan was. And because of that, Larry has come into the family and given us hope and laughter and love that we never thought we would experience; at the same time, we have changed his life, because he saw what allowing God back into our lives could do.

As I was writing this book, I spent many hours in prayer over the contents, and I felt it would not be complete without including the stories of other widows. I had asked ladies from all walks of life to write the stories of their own journeys into and through widowhood. I felt it was necessary; it would be an encouragement to others who are hurting and feel completely alone; it would remind them that everyone has their own story.

I had asked the ladies to share their journeys and to tell you how they got through them: to tell about their struggles as well as talk about the circumstances. I did not ask them to do an easy task. Writing down your feelings—opening your heart and sharing with others some of your most vulnerable thoughts—is not easy, but it does help the healing process, and it will help others. They were also to share how God was there for them when they least expected it.

So I hope you enjoy the few stories I have picked out of many to share with you. It was not an easy task to only be able to pick out these few, but I think you will see yourself, or perhaps a friend or a family member, as you read these stories from God's precious women.

I hope you enjoy these stories as much as I do and that they bring tears streaming down your face as you heal and realize the joy that God has given to you from the Holy Spirit. I pray that this book might be helpful in small way and that there are some things you might be able to identify with.

Many blessings to each of you who reads this. If you know of a widow perhaps you will think of things you can do to help in a more positive way. Ladies, if you are widows, I hope that this brings you encouragement to find purpose in your lives, because God does love you.

13

My Journey
By Peggy L.

Bobby went to be with Jesus on January 17, 2004. As I go through the healing process—through my journey of grief—I'm finding that God is always there. As I look back over the last five-and-a-half years that Bobby was sick—even on those days when things were really hard—Jesus was there: wrapping his arms of love around us, loving us through other people, special friends, and church family.

It was the summer of 1998 when we first noticed that everything was not quite right for Bobby. He began to fall asleep at work; he fell asleep twice driving home from work. He became very fatigued, and his balance was not good. He went to the doctor for what we thought was a sinus infection and got medicines, but did not get any better. So he went back to the doctor and had some blood work done. Even though his physical in May 1998 showed no problems, his blood work now began to show chronic anemia. The results of doctors' reports in the next thirty days revealed that in addition to the chronic anemia and imbalance in walking and myoclonus, chronic fatigue had become an issue. His blood pressure became extremely high, his kidneys began to function inadequately, and his thought processes became a little slower. Bobby went from working forty hours or more a week as a boilermaker-welder at TVA to being unable to work at all. He tried to work, but could not, so on July 10, 1998, he worked his last day.

I was working full-time then at the Board of Education. I would come home for lunch, prepare his lunch and mine, and then go back to work. When I came home for lunch, I would see him sitting on the couch—reading his Bible. He loved the Lord, and he loved people and loved praying for them. Bobby was a prayer warrior!

Bobby was not so weak at first, and we could do the things together that we enjoyed. We continued to go to church; we even continued to teach first-grade Sunday school together for a while—until Bobby could no longer climb the steps at church. We enjoyed just sitting on the couch together at home, drinking coffee, and talking—not about anything in particular. Just being together made us very happy. We had always spent time together in the evening, sharing stories about our day with one another. We had a very special marriage. Bobby never raised his voice to me, and I'm sure there were times that I deserved it. Jesus was the head of our home, and Bobby was the spiritual leader. We spent much time in Bible reading and prayer together. God blessed our home with love. We had two beautiful daughters who are now grown and living away from home, and they love the Lord and serve him.

The doctors were very puzzled about the proper diagnosis for Bobby's illness. In fact, they just did not know what it was. Bobby had been sick for about three years, and we were continuing to go from doctor to doctor, still without a diagnosis. One day I was praying, and I began to ask God, "Lord, what is this? Why can't the doctors figure it out? I don't know what to do. I can see Bobby getting weaker. I don't want to leave any stone unturned. What can we do?" After praying this, I felt that it was God's will for us to go to the Mayo Clinic in Rochester, Minnesota.

Some of the doctors in Nashville said to me, "They won't tell you anything there that we haven't already told you here." But I was persistent—I can be pushy when it comes to those I love! So in March 2001, we went to the Mayo Clinic.

We were at the Mayo Clinic for almost three weeks. We stayed in the Kohler Grand Hotel, which is connected to the Mayo Clinic. There was much walking to do. You could go all over the Mayo Clinic and never have to go outdoors, not even from your hotel room. On many days, we would leave our room at 7:00 AM for Bobby's appointments and not return until 5:00 PM. There were many long days at the Mayo Clinic, but God was there every step of the way! And he allowed laughter along the way—even in difficult times.

I remember one day, Bobby and I were headed to an appointment. Even though Bobby could walk at that time, all patients at the Mayo Clinic had to use wheelchairs. We were on the elevator, just minding our own business. The elevator doors opened, and I pushed Bobby forward. Well, you know that little crack of space that is at the bottom of the elevator floor? It might as well have been a huge crevice, because, as I pushed Bobby forward, for whatever reason, the front wheels of the wheelchair turned sideways and went down into the open space—and his wheelchair just got stuck. And, for some crazy reason, I just said rather loudly, "Take up thy bed and walk." I don't even know where that came from! Well, Bobby looked back at me. He got tickled, and I got tickled. We began to laugh uncontrollably, until I looked up. The doors of the elevator were still open, and there, in the lobby of this hotel, were several people staring at us! Now, this hotel was quite nice. Actually, we could not afford the hotel, but when they gave away our reserved room at the Economy Kohler because of all the bad weather and snow, we had gotten a room in this rather elegant hotel, the Kohler Grand, for the same price. God is good!

As these people were staring at us, they were trying to figure out what other problems we had, in addition to a medical problem. It was very obvious that they thought we were crazy! So, embarrassed as I was, I jerked on the wheelchair. It became free, and I pulled Bobby back and pushed another button...any button. Boy, was I glad that the door closed! We waited for what seemed like minutes (it was actually only seconds) until the door opened again. And yes, you guessed it: I had pushed the wrong button, and there were the same people on the same floor, staring at us...again. By this time, it was no longer funny. I just ducked my head, said, "Hold on," and pushed with all my might to get off of the elevator and go anywhere out of sight of the lobby. This, of course, was one of Bobby's favorite stories to tell all the relatives when we got home!

Another story he liked to tell was about when we actually left the Mayo Clinic one afternoon when he didn't have any appointments. We were headed for a store that sold wheelchairs. If Bobby needed one, I wanted to be sure that we could order one that would be comfortable and would fit his needs. We had gone on a shuttle from the Mayo Clinic to the Methodist hospital just a few blocks away, had lunch in the cafeteria there, and then set out for the wheelchair store. We were on our own now for transportation. Since it wasn't far, we just decided to walk. Well, I walked; Bobby rode. We came to a place where I could see the store just across the way. So I said, "Hang on—we'll hurry across the street in between the traffic." Well, I hurried too much. I got us across the street, and there was a tiny step up—ever so slight. But I didn't see it! When I hit the "ever-so-slight" step up, I thought Bobby was going to catapult into space. He hollered, and I grabbed him and kept him in the chair. Then we started laughing. After the stress at the Mayo Clinic, anything became funny; we were so tired by this time. I do remember, though, Bobby complaining just a little about my "driving skills," at which I offered to trade places. He very quickly decided that I was the best driver that he had ever had!

We did manage to come away from the Mayo Clinic with a diagnosis that was close, but not totally accurate. It was only after coming back home and going to a doctor of genetics at Vanderbilt University Medical Center that we received the actual diagnosis. Bobby also had many doctors at St. Thomas Hospital. It was while going to the doctors' appointments at St. Thomas that I was allowed to perfect my "wheelchair driving." I remember one of the first times that I pushed Bobby to his doctor's appointment. It seemed that I hit every door facing there. I couldn't judge my distance very well. After bumping into six or eight doors, I remember Bobby making the comment to the nurse, "I think we've got the wrong one on the table," while rolling his eyes toward me. The doctors and nurses all loved him—he never lost his sense of humor.

After going to a doctor of genetics at Vanderbilt University Medical Center and receiving the actual diagnosis, our journey became more serious. Bobby was diagnosed with a muscle and cell disorder, a mitochondrial disease: cell mutation number 8344. The disease was progressive, but because it was so rare and very few people in the entire world had ever had this diagnosis, there was no research on it. Almost nothing was known about this particular disease. So our prayer was that the progressive part of the disease would be very slow. Bobby had carried this mutation all his life, but it was not until he was fifty years old that the disease had manifested itself.

But God brings good even out of sad situations. The disease that Bobby had was a maternally inherited disease. Bobby and twenty-five of his relatives participated in the first research that had ever been done on the 8344 mutation. And, because of this research and future research, someday a couple will have a child, the child will have this disease, and the child will live—all because of the love of people who cared and participated in research to help someone else.

God continued to take care of us over the next couple of years. He met our every need. Then, on January 6, 2004, Bobby went into the hospital at St. Thomas. This was the first time during his five-and-a-half-year illness that he had to be hospitalized. I began to keep a journal several years ago and continued to do so, even at the hospital. I later felt that God wanted me to type up my journal notes from the hospital. He actually impressed that upon me just a few months after Bobby died, but I just couldn't do it then. So I waited and just recently, God reminded me again and again, so I obeyed him and typed up the hospital notes. At the beginning of the hospital stay, I thought we were only going to be there a couple of days, so I just jotted journal notes on napkins, pieces of paper, whatever I had. But somehow, God preserved all those little notes, and, when it came time to put them on paper, I had them all—another one of his miracles.

God was faithful to us all throughout the hospital stay. He put people in our path to minister to us, and even on several occasions allowed us to minister to others there in the hospital. I remember one particular instance. It was actually on the morning of the day that Bobby died. I felt in my heart on the morning of January 17, 2004, that God was letting me know that this was going to be the day that Bobby was going home to be with Jesus! I called my best friend and my sister and told them this was going to be Bobby's home-going day. I just felt it in my heart. And, because I felt it so strongly, at about 7:30 AM, I packed up the room completely, and then I just sat beside Bobby's bed and prayed and read my Bible. God was so close to me that morning and even led me to certain passages in the Bible that were of such comfort to me. I remember writing the passages on a napkin, which was my paper at the time. After the room was packed up and I had finished my Bible reading in Psalms and prayed, I just sat there feeling very sad as I reflected on the past days and pondered what today would bring. I thought about how I had prayed with Bobby as he was getting worse and had explained to him that if he was too weak to breathe properly (his chest muscles were too weak to exhale the carbon dioxide properly), he would go on to heaven to be with Jesus. I told him that God must have something else for me to do—that I hadn't accomplished God's plan for my life, so I couldn't go to heaven with him now. And then I assured him that I would be there later, and he could watch for me. Oh, what a day that will be!

As I think back to that morning of January 17, 2004, I remember an incident that occurred, and I remember finding more paper to write it down so I would be able to share it with the kids later. At 8:10 AM, Dr. A. came by to check on Bobby. Dr. A. also said that he wanted to share something privately with me. He said that the other day, when he had talked with me in the emergency room, he had felt something he had never felt before. When he had told me how sick Bobby was, he had seen himself in my face.

One morning in December 2003, he had been feeding breakfast to his fifteen-month-old son, and then just two hours later, he was dead. He didn't give me any details, but I could tell it had been sudden. He was not angry at God, but he said he was confused. He said that eternity is forever and that he would see his son again. There were two doctors working on his son, but he still had died. He had the option of putting his son on a ventilator, which would have kept him alive a long time, but not in a natural state. When I told him that keeping Bobby alive mechanically was selfish—only for our sake—he just rubbed his head and said that that was exactly what he had told his son's doctor. He said that God's will has to be done! God's will has to be done! I shared with him how God sees the big puzzle of life, and how we only make up the small puzzle pieces. He nodded.

It was totally amazing that God had sent this Christian doctor to Bobby's bedside to minister to me as I was sitting there overwhelmed with sadness. Dr. A. stood up and said, "Give me a hug—you're going to make me cry."

I told him how sorry I was for his loss. He said that he wished we could have had more time together—Bobby and I—but I told him how God had been so gracious in giving us those last twelve days at the hospital together with Robin and Mandy and Matt, and how special those times had been. He said that he probably shouldn't be talking to me like this, but I said, "That's okay—we're Christians, and that's what we do!"

Dr. A. asked me if I wanted him to try to wake Bobby up. I said, "No, let's just let God's will happen." I told him that Bobby had been sleeping for a long time, and that I didn't know if he would wake up again.

God provided much comfort and strength through close friends, family, and our church family. The last twelve days of Bobby's life were some of the hardest days I've ever experienced. Our kids were there, and our best friends were there all through this time. We just hung onto Jesus; he brought us through. I guess the sweetest thing God allowed was that just moments before Bobby died on January 17, 2004, he smiled. Our daughters and I saw it! I just thanked Jesus for that sweet smile, but I told him, "Even without that smile, Jesus, I would have known he'd be with you!"

God wants to take the most painful experience in our lives and turn them around to his honor and glory. We know from the Scriptures that God is near the brokenhearted; he binds up our wounds; he will sustain us. He even collects our tears, as in a wineskin. God is the healer of broken hearts. He invites us to rest in the shadow of the Almighty—just think how close you have to be to someone to be in his shadow. And God invites us to be right there!

After Bobby went to heaven, I continued to write in my journal. I carried my journal to the cemetery, and I remember saying to Bobby one day that one of the things I missed the most was not being able to just talk to him and tell him about everything. I missed his love and his touch. I just missed being with him. I was very sad, and I felt like my heart was going to explode. So I decided that I would continue to record my thoughts in my journal, as if I were sharing with Bobby the things going on in my life. It has helped me so much, and God has used my own writings to minister back to me as I read them over from time to time and see his faithfulness. I realize that he has blessed me so much: what Bobby and I had was more precious than words can describe. And our Heavenly Father is the one who provided that for us!

One of the things that I began to pray about after Bobby's passing was, "Lord, what now? Lord, Bobby and I did everything together…I don't know what I'm going to do now…I feel incomplete…I feel like half a person. Lord, please help me!" One of the first things God impressed upon me was that one is complete in him and that he could make me whole again!

I had recently read *Purpose-Driven Life* by Rick Warren, and I knew that God still had a purpose for this new season of my life as I began this journey of grief. I just didn't have a clue at that point in my life what that might be!

My daughters and I attended a Women of Faith conference in Nashville, Tennessee, in April 2004. As God would have it, the title of the conference was Irrepressible Hope. They even addressed grief and death. Tammy Trent, a nationally known singer and entertainer, was one of the guest speakers. She spoke about losing her husband, Trent, in a scuba-diving accident the day before the tragedy of September 11. She spoke about her love for Trent and how God was holding her up during this time of sorrow. She shared from her heart that day, and God ministered to me through her testimony. It was from her Web site that God led my daughter to the Web site of Widow2Widow™.

I had never heard of Widow2Widow™, but at the persistent nudging of my daughter, I finally checked it out. When I went to the Web site, I decided to e-mail Elaine Cook, the founder and president. This is not what I normally do when I go to a Web page, but for some reason—I guess it was because I was having such a sad morning—I e-mailed Elaine. That was at 11:02 AM on August 22, 2004. At 1:35 PM on the same day, Elaine e-mailed me back with words of encouragement. Boy, was I surprised to get such a quick response! Later, after getting to know Elaine, I realized that this was so much a part of her character. She has such a passion for the hurting widow!

Going to the Widow2Widow™ Web page not only introduced me to Elaine Cook, but it also made me aware of the first-ever annual retreat for widows that was scheduled in Carson Springs Baptist Conference Center, Newport, Tennessee, for September 2–4, 2004. As I read on, I realized that the closing date for registration had already passed, so I figured that was out for me. Wrong! God had another plan. In a matter of four days, God had pulled it all together so that I could go to the retreat—I was able to register, I was able to take off from work, transportation was provided, and my church was totally supportive of me. There was nothing lacking; I was going to the retreat! I have to admit that my reasons for going to the retreat were purely selfish. I was hurting; I was concerned about my broken heart and shattered life. But here again, God had another plan. It was during the retreat and on the way back home on the bus that God impressed upon me that this retreat was not all about me. He wanted me to take this time of refreshing and healing and use it to minister to others. I wasn't sure what this meant, but I learned later that I was in for the ride of my life! Nothing is ever dull when serving the Lord!

I must tell you about my retreat experiences! I really was not crazy about driving to Brentwood Baptist Church that morning, boarding a bus with ladies I didn't know, riding to East Tennessee, and having a roommate whom I'd never met—and for two nights at that. Boy, was I stepping out of the box. My comfort zone was so far behind, I couldn't even remember how it felt! I was definitely challenged that day. Plus, I forgot to mention, it was pouring down rain and I got lost—it seemed like a good reason to back out. But then I knew I'd have to explain to God why. So I prayed, "Lord, you know I'm lost. If you want me to get there, then you'll have to help me." It wasn't a very spiritual prayer, but it worked. God did want me on that bus, and he helped me find my way.

This is where God's humor began to show! I made it fine onto the bus with the ladies. They were kind and warm and made me feel very welcome. I was thinking to myself: *So, great, the bus ride will be over soon…I can't wait to meet my roommate…who knows, maybe she won't show…maybe I'll have a room to myself.* I don't think my attitude was bad; I was just uncomfortable. I was definitely being stretched by a God who was supposed to love me. My roommate did show up. Her name was Carol Marie. Not only did she show up, she brought half her belongings with her. I later found out that it was because she was into makeup, makeovers, hairstyling, and all that other stuff. This still didn't impress me, because I'm not into all that stuff, but people like that have fun with people like me. Well, I met her at dinner that night. When I won a prize, I went up to get it, and someone said, "Oh, Peggy, hi, I'm your roommate."

I thought, "Dear Lord, I'm not anything like she is. This lady is so different from me, it's not even funny." But, it was—I didn't know that I was going to get a foot massage, a haircut, and a makeover all in one retreat. But God's humor turned very tender when I got to know my roommate a little better and realized that she loved the Lord with all her heart and that she used her God-given talents to minister to hurting widows. She was one of the keynote speakers at the retreat. God is so good, and he ministered to me through my new friend, Carol Marie. We spent time in prayer together and just sharing our hearts and sharing the pain in our lives with each other. I really needed this, because I had only been a widow for about seven months. Carol Marie was widowed about five years before. It was at this retreat that I learned that it's okay to laugh again. God approves of laughter, even through the pain.

I enjoyed the retreat in many other ways as well. The fellowship with the other ladies was very healing. The time of praise and worship was awesome! The speakers just spoke directly to my heart. Some of the topics that were shared were about the eagle: how God takes care of us like he does the eagle, and how the eagle flies through the storm and doesn't give up. There was a message about embracing life, in which we were encouraged to go forward in our lives in service to God. Another message was on the plight of widows: how God views the widow, how widows have a place of honor in God's sight, how he loves them, and how we, as widows, are called to the prayer ministry as prayer warriors. That's one of God's purposes for us in this new season of our lives.

After I returned home from the retreat, I began to pray and ask for direction for my life. As God would have it, his new plan for this new season of my life, this journey of grief, would be for me to help start a Widow2Widow™ ministry for my own church and community. We had the support of our pastors, the women's ministry, and many friends—and, of course, the widows that God began to place in my life immediately upon my return home from the retreat. I was so touched to see how quickly this ministry came together. God is truly in it!

Our first Widow2Widow™ meeting was on November 13, 2004. We had twenty-three widows—only six of them were from our church; the others were from the community. Elaine Cook was our special guest speaker and spoke about how the ministry came about. I gave a short testimony as well. Given the fact that stage fright is something I've battled for years, I was not sure this would go well—I feared I might throw up or worse! But God is gracious. He intended for this to glorify him, and it did!

Our local Widow2Widow™ meeting is once a month on a Saturday morning. We have special guest speakers who speak on different topics of interest for widows. We fellowship and eat together. We do mission projects together. We meet every week or so at the local restaurant for coffee or dinner. We do all of this to minister to one another as widow to widow and woman to woman. God honors this ministry because he is working in our hearts as we serve him and reach out to each other. There is such comfort in walking this journey with someone who knows how it feels to be brokenhearted, how it feels to have your dreams and life shattered, how it feels to have that piercing pain go through your heart, and how if feels to just be overwhelmed with sadness. It's a comfort to have someone walk alongside you as you walk this journey. As God begins to heal our broken hearts, he wants us to reach out to someone else and be there for them.

God has not healed my broken heart completely. He can—I know he can. But somehow, as I'm broken and crushed, I've come to depend upon him more and more. And as God takes me through this season of grief, it's much like the Scripture in Luke 12:48 (KJV) that says, "For unto whomsoever much is given, of him shall be much required." As God has ministered to me this last year, he has given me much love, comfort, strength, and the will to go on living. God has given so much to me, and much will be required as I continue to heal and serve him. God has called me to minister to the hurting—specifically, the hurting widows and their children. And I'm doing that through the Widow2Widow™ ministry.

I'm not here to pretend that I don't still have a tremendous amount of pain in my heart—I do…I still do. I don't understand a lot of things. But early on in my grief, I learned in a Bible study that I don't have to know the "why" if I know the "who." And I know the "who"—he's Jesus Christ!

I pray that if you have any pain in your life, from whatever source, that you will join me in giving it all to Jesus. There's just something about that name. When I feel a sharp pain from loss, I just look up and say, "Jesus, I love you." He's as close as the whisper of his name.

So enjoy the day! Hold the ones you love *so* very close, and allow God, the father of all comfort, to minister to you. Let Jesus love you! And press on to the high calling God has put before you—don't give up!

14

My Journey
By Josette M.

Three-and-a-half years ago, if anyone had told me I would soon be a widow, I would have told them it was not going to happen. I lived, confident and secure, in the belief that my husband would live well into his nineties, as did his parents. It wasn't to be. After just seven weeks of battling acute leukemia, he died on July 15, 2001. My journey as a widow began on that day.

After spending many days and nights at the hospital, it was easy to convince myself that I needed to go to bed and stay there. I had no energy and lacked direction for months after his death, fluctuating between despair and grief, to pleading with God to help me with the pain of excruciating loneliness. As most women who have faced life without their best friend, I soon realized that life goes on. For example, financial decisions have to be made, the will has to be probated, the yard needs mowing, the car has to be maintained, the house needs repairs, and with every change that is made, someone needs a copy of the death certificate.

During this time, I began to write prayers to the Lord. I kept a journal, and at the end of each day, I told Jesus my thoughts and emotions. This has been very valuable in chronicling my journey. I began to thank him for taking care of me, for paving the way in difficult situations, for showing me I could do things I had never done before, and for giving me opportunities of service to others. I learned that I could reach out to others that were hurting with compassion I had never experienced before. I thanked him especially for my family, for special friends who comforted me, for the books compassionate people shared with me, and especially for the opportunities to serve in various capacities in my church.

Several months after my husband's death, I was invited to attend a support group in my church entitled Grief/Share. I stayed in Grief/Share for two years, helping to facilitate each new group. These groups were made up of people who had lost loved ones. In January 2004, together with a friend (also a widow), I began a Widow2Widow™ ministry at Green Acres Baptist Church in Tyler, Texas. Somewhere on our journeys, God gave us a heart for widows. With the encouragement and prayers of Elaine Cook, the founder of Widow2Widow™, we are beginning our second year of leading this special group of women.

My journey is not over. I still miss my husband every day. Only as I walk with Jesus and surrender myself to him daily am I able to feel that I am not alone. God is faithful. "He is able to do immeasurably more than all we ask or imagine according to his power that is at work within us" (Ephesians 3:20).

He is with us every step of the way on this journey through widowhood.

15

My Journey:
The Extreme Makeover
by Carol Marie S.

Sonny was my Southern gentleman from Tennessee, born on the fourth of July. Now, for a California girl, that was romantic! I graduated from high school in June, married Sonny on Labor Day weekend in September, and started beauty school two weeks later! Dad was a career military man, which made me an Air Force brat (though my mother assures me that I always was delightful). We traveled a lot (which I enjoyed), but when I could, I visited my grandma, who was a cosmetologist. The first haircut I did was on my sister when I was four and she was only one. (She was also the first "skinhead.") Mom was relieved that I hadn't cut her, and she realized that there must be some talent in there somewhere. My brother was older and quicker and was able to hide his curly locks from me. Later, Mom and I had a skin-care and makeup business when I was fifteen and sixteen, so Grandma's genes must have gotten into me. I loved doing makeovers and seeing others feel better about themselves.

Sonny thought I was the best thing since sliced bread! I was raised in a Christian home, and I made sure Sonny believed in God as our courting became more serious. Sonny smoked, but I was used to that with my dad, so I didn't think much about it. He also enjoyed beer, but it never seemed that it would be a problem. Everyone liked Sonny; he was the big brother that many wished they had. He always had the ability to see good in you, and he would never put you down, even if you deserved it. He was always fun to be with, and I felt honored that he had chosen me to spend his life with.

Throughout our thirty-four years of marriage, I continued to work with hair, skin care, and makeup in a salon that later grew into a day-spa business. His enjoyment of beer increased as the pressures grew with his job and our family. Without realizing it, I enabled his lifestyle. I went to the kids' activities and to most church and family functions alone. Sonny seemed very supportive of my dreams because he loved me. He loved his children as well, but he had a dependency that controlled most of his life. Though I had a relationship with the Lord, I tended to lose myself in work in order to cope with stress and issues. I was taught as a child: "If you can't say something nice, don't say anything at all!" I didn't deal with things; I just made it look pretty and acceptable. Sonny would start drinking as soon as he got home from work and stop right before he ate dinner and went to bed. He always acted lovingly toward our two children and me, but he just numbed himself to life—and therefore, to us.

I filled the loneliness with work. Because I could not control what was going on with Sonny, I tried to control what I did have control over: employees, children, and work. With hard work, the business seemed to flourish. Partners came on board as we branched out into the day-spa world. Opportunities opened up for radio, television, and important positions in the community. I was writing for a health magazine and writing beauty columns for the newspaper. I trained staff, developed products, and worked with clients. I thought I was Superwoman, wearing so many hats and keeping everything going. It was looking good. I had worked for twenty years to birth this business. It was like a child, and I watched it grow. We had put every penny we had into it, for we planned it to be our retirement.

In 1998, through a series of events, our business partners shrewdly transferred the assets into their names and the debt into Sonny's and mine. Before the end of the year, the spa was closed, and my heart was ripped out of me. Superwoman had lost her cape! The stress was almost unbearable for Sonny. I could not understand what was happening...my dreams had crumbled before my eyes. Overnight I went from having recognition and value to feeling worthless and being accused of things of which I had no knowledge. Attorneys advised us that there was nothing we could do. I was in a state of shock and disbelief. Guilt clutched my heart, as I knew I should have been wiser. During this humbling time, I began doing consulting work out of our home. It gave me time with Sonny, and opportunities to try to reestablish our relationship that had grown so far apart. It was a time of seeking the Lord to find out who I was, instead of what my titles had portrayed.

Sonny loved to fish from our back patio, and I would watch him...and even cook the ones he caught! We would sit by the water, and he would sing to me and play his guitar. (This was my dream home, the one I had sketched on a napkin twenty-five years before. We had found it and enjoyed it for four years, but with the closing of the spa, we could not continue to keep it.) I loved him and wanted to see him free. I began to go to a Christian twelve-step program and invited

Sonny to join me. It was for those with all types of addictions and their families. Sonny refused to go, saying that he and the Lord could handle it. I continued going, knowing that I needed insight for both Sonny's and my needs. Later, I visited family in Tennessee and tried an intervention to force him to get help with the drinking issue. The stress from closing the spa, the overwhelming bills, and Sonny's history of turning to beer to cope only increased the problem.

On the Sunday right before Thanksgiving 1999, Sonny could not breathe and needed to be taken to the emergency room. He had gotten the flu and it had turned into bronchitis. My friend Maggie, who was a nurse, warned me that coming off alcohol quickly could cause complications. Her husband used to drink with Sonny, so she knew of his consumption. Through a chain of events, complications did take place, ending with dementia.

He was released to go home. Sonny knew us sometimes, and sometimes he did not. He was confused and had to be watched continually. The guys from Victory Outreach offered to help me. They prayed over him daily and took turns watching him with me, so he wouldn't run off or hurt himself. During this time, Sonny was set free from alcohol and cigarettes. He recommitted his life to the Lord and would even preach to the chairs, the tables, and me. I was so sure that he would be totally healed and his mind would be restored. I had visions of us sharing the gospel all over the world, now that our lives were back on track.

On Christmas Eve, I was nervous. I had no help with him—the guys at Victory Outreach had plans for the holiday. We had been invited to our families' homes, but the confusion Sonny was in made it impossible. I cried out for help from the Lord, and surprisingly, Christmas Eve went smoothly, with no episodes! On Christmas morning, as we sat at the dining-room table and I was helping him with his breakfast, Sonny turned to me and said, "Who is that over there?"

I said, "Over where?" Sonny motioned with his head, nodding towards the doorway to the kitchen.

I asked Sonny what it looked like. After looking for a moment, he said, "Well, he's sixteen feet tall!"

I said, "Do you think it is an angel?"

Sonny looked more closely this time, looked up and down, and then said, "Yep! He's an angel!" I thought: no wonder Sonny was acting so well. I cried out for help, and God sent me an angel!

On the day after Christmas, Sonny began to run a fever. He had fallen a couple of weeks earlier and had been taken to the emergency room to have a place on his head sewn up. I wondered if it might be a reaction to something they had given him. I admitted Sonny on Monday, and on Tuesday they determined that he had picked up a staph infection. It had gone through his body, and they were unable to stop it.

On Wednesday, as I prayed at the foot of Sonny's bed, I heard the Lord say to me, "Can you trust him to me totally?" I knew what he meant: whether he stayed here on earth or went to heaven—whether he came back to me mentally or was healed.

God was not just talking about Sonny's future, but mine as well. The doctor had already spoken to me of Sonny's need to go to a place where he could get care, for we could not continue like we had been doing. After some thought—for I knew that I had to answer from my heart—I said, "Yes, Lord. You are in control. Whether he stays or goes, you know what is right. I trust you." At 4:30 PM, Sonny moved to heaven.

My journey through grief included four years of fog. I think I just shut down inside. Then I began to start feeling again. I had anger toward the alcohol and toward Sonny for letting it rob him of his family, life and intimacy with me. I had anger toward myself for being an enabler. I had guilt, wishing I had done things differently. I even felt guilty for not feeling more pain over my loss of him. I knew that I loved him, but I was used to doing things alone. So when I saw others who lost a spouse fall apart, I wondered what was wrong with me. A licensed counselor told me that I had been grieving for years before Sonny had died. He told me that all grief journeys are different, and each person's grief is unique. The stages may be the same, but how we go through them varies. Grief happens when loss occurs, and loss can be experienced in many forms. It can be through the loss of a loved one, a relationship, a job, a career, a ministry, or even a dream you counted on. When you have more than one of these areas of loss, complicated grief occurs. This helped me to take time to heal and to avoid comparing myself with others.

Since most of the holidays were connected to Sonny in some way—Father's Day, the Fourth of July, Labor Day, Thanksgiving, Christmas, and New Year's—I have had to create new memories instead of feeling bad about the old ones. I look for new ways to celebrate, and for those who need a fresh memory to share it with! Maybe this will be helpful for you too. For though I did things alone most of the time, Sonny was always at home. Going to bed alone has probably been the hardest thing for me.

I was used to going to experts to find answers for my clients. I had worked on famous faces with NBC-TV that needed to look their best. Now I faced new questions concerning *my* life and future…and I needed the ultimate expert! I began to spend more time with God in prayer, asking him about everything…giving him everything…trusting him with everything! He began to reveal the selfish areas of my life, the controlling spirit I had picked up. He showed me how greed and pride had opened the door for the pain I had experienced in the business world, and why I had been deceived. I repented and asked him to restore my life!

God is still doing an "extreme makeover" of my life! It's not happening over-night, for extreme ones take time.

I live and work at a widows' center in ministry, and, yes, I do makeovers on the ladies! As I humble myself, God has given me opportunities to write for a magazine, do guest appearances on television, and even house-sit a condo on the water! God is giving back to me everything I have loved. I travel with mission trips, see people all over the world, and share the love of Jesus. I enjoy my children, and my grandkids have special times with them. Best of all, God has become my husband, like Isaiah talks about.

I decided to walk in F.O.G. instead of fog! That's walking in the Favor Of God! I teach others to see their position in him as well. Not because of who we are in ourselves, but because of who he is in us! Yes, there is an "extreme make-over" that only the ultimate expert can do, and he's still doing it on me and will do it for you as well!

16

Widow Story
By Gayle H.

I became a widow at forty-nine years old, and this is my story.

Frank and I met in the summer of 1979, but we did not start dating until that fall. We dated for six months, fell in love, and got married. We were twenty-six years old, and I remember when we talked about how we might not see our fiftieth wedding anniversary, but knew we would celebrate our twenty-fifth. It never happened.

A week before Thanksgiving, God called Frank home. We had been married for twenty-four years. For our twenty-fifth wedding anniversary, we had made plans to renew our vows in the presence of God, our two sons, and our family. Instead, I was alone on our anniversary and spent the day crying and being depressed, wondering what had gone wrong and why would God do this.

Frank and I loved one another and still do. We have two sons that we love. Our marriage wasn't perfect; we had our share of troubles, like everyone else does. I just called it life. We had our struggles and calamities, death and despair, but there was happiness, joy, and lots of comedy too. I had always felt well-rounded, normal.

It has been a year now, and how do I feel? I guess you could say well-rounded—normal, if there is such a thing as being normal. During this time, I have found out that I can survive, and, as they say, life does go on, and I have, but with struggles.

Frank died at home in our bed between 1:00 AM and 3:00 AM. My son found him. I remember it like it was yesterday. I remember the doctor at the hospital telling me he was gone and asking him if he was sure. I asked if they had done everything and said to take me back there so I could make sure they had tried. But they wouldn't let me go back.

I remember thinking, please don't let him die. But it was too late: heaven was calling.

I was in shock for what seemed to be an eternity, but it was only about six months. I don't remember the funeral or who attended. I don't remember the cards or phone calls or the thank-you notes or the food brought to the house. I do remember the pain. I do remember how my world seemed to stop. I remember the ache in my heart as it was ripping apart. I now understand the phrase, "died from a broken heart." I stayed in shock or disbelief. I cried, I screamed; I talked to God, I screamed at God; I was angry, sad, lonely, miserable, and unhappy. I wanted to die and even contemplated it. That is when I knew I needed help.

The doctor said that I was depressed. It was as if someone had opened up the floodgates, and I could not stop crying for months. They performed stress tests to see if there was something wrong with my heart. You see, I was dying of a broken heart.

I was willing myself to die. I actually thought I could do it, since God had abandoned me. *Wrong.* This was the turning point.

The doctor gave me pills for depression, which I took, but taking them was causing me to be "slap-happy." I thought I'd had one too many drinks or something. I didn't like the effects the medication had on my body, so I quit taking it. Instead of taking it every day, I would tell myself six or more times a day, "I can do all things in Christ, who strengthens me."

Slowly, oh, so slowly, I am making it back. Inch by inch. Am I there yet? Will I ever be? I just don't know. But what I do know is that without counseling, support groups, friends, family, and God, I would have given up on life. Do I still have moments of craziness, fear, panic, loneliness, and great sadness? Oh, yes—but I can do all things in Christ, who strengthens me.

And some day, when it's "my time," God will take me home, and we will be together again. It will be well-rounded and wonderful.

17

When I Became a Widow
January 30, 2001
By Karen S.

I met Mitchell during a time in my life when I was running away from God. I had been through an abusive marriage that ended in divorce and left me with four young boys between the ages of three and thirteen; Robbie, Billy, Tommy, and Michael. I had been struggling for about three years, when one night I cried to the Lord to help me accept being alone for the rest of my life, raising my boys, and growing old without someone to hug me. Then along came Mitch. He had been through some nasty trials. His first wife had been murdered, leaving him with a three-year-old (Michael also known as "Big Mike"); and then he had been with a wife who had told him after twenty years of marriage that she didn't like being married to a pastor and wanted a divorce. They had three children: Sidney, Debbie, and Paul. They were all grown and on their own. Mitch was nine years older than I was.

We dated for about three years before he decided that we should get married. He very politely asked me one night if I would like to get married. I answered, "Yes, that would be nice." When he asked when, I told him, "Yesterday would have been nice," but we settled on a wedding date and moved on.

We had a wonderfully blessed marriage. There were some ups and downs and some extremely difficult times, but with God's guiding hand, we always made it through the good times and the bad. Mitch was my *rock* when Robbie was killed in a motorcycle accident and when my mother was diagnosed with Alzheimer's Disease. He was right there for me.

He was a very robust man: always smiling…twinkling blue eyes…white hair and a beard. Yes, he portrayed Santa Claus. He was always careful not to promise any gift for Christmas and to always ask the children where they went to Sunday school. He successfully did the "Santa thing" for about five years. Then on December 23, 1998, when he came home from "North Pole duty," he was really sick. He had picked up some flu bug and a cold from some of the little ones and thought he just needed to get some extra rest. But when he tried to sleep that night he began having problems catching his breath.

At about 3:30 AM on December 24, 1998, he woke me and gasped that he needed some help breathing. I jumped up and dressed, woke Michael, and we rushed him to the hospital. When we got there, they hooked him up to all kinds of machines and started running tests. By 6:00 AM they didn't know for sure what the real problem was, but they did know he had pneumonia and he was admitted. He was taken to the cardiac intensive care unit (CICU), because of the short staff for the holidays.

By 2:00 PM that day, they had finally diagnosed that he had streptococcal pneumonia and streptococcal sepsis. (That is like strep throat of the lungs and strep throat throughout the entire blood system—not a good situation.) He was on a respirator/ventilator and all kinds of other machines. They took X-rays, blood tests, EKGs, EEGs, and all the other letter names they could put together. They also called in a specialist. His kidneys had begun to shut down…he was dying. The doctor was very kind when he told me I should call all the family members to come home

Christmas Eve, 1998: what a day to remember. I began calling all the kids. Big Mike and Elaine were in North Carolina, Sidney had gone to Fulton and Deb was there as well, Paul and Cess were in Oklahoma City, and Billy and Cheri had come to the hospital. Tom was in England, and Michael was at the hospital. I also called Mitch's sister in Colorado and his brother, who was in Columbia. I knew some of them would be traveling and perhaps be close to Springfield, but I did not expect the response I got from most of them. To begin with, Sid had his cell phone turned off and I couldn't reach him. Paul's phone had been disconnected. I got Tom out of bed in England. Bill and Cheri and Michael were already there, but the rest replied, "Well, this is Christmas Eve, so we are on our way to church. We'll add him to our prayer list and see how he is tomorrow." I was really upset, but decided it wasn't worth letting it get to me; it was their choice. Of course, I had called our church family, and the pastor had been there, and oodles of people came in and out all day, and even on Christmas Day they came in and out.

After about forty-eight hours on the respirator, he began to show marked improvement, and the prognosis was recovery, but it would take some time. He was on the respirator for just hours short of ten days and was in the hospital for another week, and then in a nursing home/rehab center for about two weeks. I had gone back to work and Mitch was at home recovering when I got a call that my mother had passed away. On January 25, 1999, I got everything ready and we all headed to Minnesota to make arrangements and have a funeral for Mom.

Mitch was there all the way for me, of course, even though he was still a bit weak. Little did I know, at the time, that he was as well as he was going to be. From then on, his health deteriorated. That summer, he began having problems breathing again. They diagnosed him with CHF and COPD—more letters (congestive heart failure and chronic obstructive pulmonary disease). There were other problems too, but these were the major issues. He did pretty well for the next ten or eleven months, and then the breathing problems got worse. He was in and out of the hospital four or five times in about four months and was always on oxygen at home.

During this time, I was still working as the receptionist at American Dehydrated Foods, Inc., in Springfield, Missouri. I had been there for sixteen years, and they were considerate of the stress I was going through. I was reassured by the verse in Philippians 4:13 where God promises: "I can do all things through Him who strengthens me." I would get up at about 4:00 AM to get ready for work, then go take care of Mitch. Since he couldn't breathe when he lay down, he slept on the couch sitting up. I took care of his immediate needs, changed his clothes for the day, got his breakfast ready, and fed it to him because he was so weak and couldn't always get the food to his mouth. I would prepare a snack for him to eat during the morning, then I would hurry off to work so I would be there by 7:30 AM. At noon, I would leave the office, drive twenty minutes back home, take care of my sweetheart, fix his lunch, feed him (another twenty minutes), and hurry back to work. Three days a week, I would meet the home health care nurse there on my lunch hour to evaluate his condition. Then on January 22, 2001, the home health care nurse called me at work to tell me my husband needed to be in the hospital again. I left work at a run and drove home (though I don't really remember driving). The nurse made the necessary phone calls to the doctor, the ambulance came, and we raced to the hospital one more time.

The doctors in the emergency room all knew us by this time, so after many examinations, consultations, tests, and so on, they determined that there was nothing more they could do for him—*but* he could not stay in the hospital unless they could do some medical procedure on him. They basically told me insurance would not cover another stay unless they cut him. After that final consultation with the doctor, Mitch asked me what they were going to do. When I told him, he was quiet for a few minutes, then said, "I just don't understand why God won't let me get better." My only reply was that I felt this was God's way of telling us that he would be taking him home soon. He thought that one through, then smiled sweetly and said, "Well, I don't want to leave you, but I'll be waiting for you to come join me." We both cried.

That night, they took him back to the nursing home where he stayed for four days. He was growing weaker by the day, and on Friday I got a call telling me that he needed to go back to the hospital. I ran to the nursing home, they made the call for an ambulance, Sidney got there, Billy and Cheri and Michael all got there, and off we went to the hospital.

This time they admitted him to the medical intensive care unit (MICU) and let me stay with him to help feed him and just be with him. He became weaker by the hour but was still hanging on, and on Sunday afternoon they moved him to a private room at the corner of the medical ward. Since it was on the corner, it was bigger and could hold more people. By this time, I had called all the family members and told them they had better make immediate plans to come home if they wanted to see him alive one more time. On Sunday night he had a seizure, and I thought he was gone, but God gave him to me for a few more hours. On Monday, the family started making plans to arrive, and each time they called, I told him which one would be there soon. He was semiconscious by this time, but he always smiled when I talked to him. He would always try to hug me—that was our favorite way of communicating, and, believe me, I really miss those hugs.

On Monday night, Sidney decided to stay at the hospital with me, and we sort of catnapped off and on. At about 3:30 AM on Tuesday, January 30, 2001, we both startled when we heard a gasp and a breath. The nurse came in, checked his vitals, and told both of us she had to get another nurse for a second opinion before he could be pronounced deceased—but he had just passed away. We started calling the local family, our church family, the pastor, and the distant family members. Billy and Cheri and Michael were there within minutes. The others completed their travel plans and came in at different times on Tuesday and Wednesday.

We finally got ourselves together, and they guided me out to the car and back home. I made a few phone calls, then slept on the couch for a couple of hours. Friends called, came by the house, brought food, hugged us, and cried with us. I am not sure who it was, but someone picked up the house and cleaned the kitchen, I think…I just don't know who.

We made the arrangements for his funeral to be on Friday with a visitation on Thursday evening. His sister flew in from Colorado; his brother came in from Columbia, Missouri; Big Mike and Elaine drove in from North Carolina; Tom flew in from England; and the others all got there sometime and some way. I sort of spent the week in a fog, trying to make arrangement and decisions and to just get through each day. I could feel God's presence in everything I did, everything I said, and everything I thought I said. He was there with me in spirit, through friends, family, neighbors, and everyone that called. There were so many plants and flowers delivered to the house that it seemed like a greenhouse. One of the most special plants was one sent by the doctor who had first cared for him in the ER, Dr. Thomas Woodward, when he was diagnosed with pneumonia.

From that time on, I had known that my husband was going to die. It was just a feeling, I guess. There were no lights or great revelations from God, just the quiet instinct that he was preparing me to be alone.

When Mitch died, I was tired and worn out from the stress of caring for him, keeping him comfortable, getting his medication, feeding him, bathing him, changing him, finding time for me to spend with him and for us to spend with God, keeping the house clean, getting the laundry done, and, of course, working. I almost felt a sigh of relief, but I also felt a *big* empty hole in my life—not just my heart, my *life*. What was I going to do? We had planned for me to retire (quit working?) when I turned sixty so we could do some traveling. Our dream had been to drive to Alaska. I just knew that it would never happen. I would have to work until I died. I cried and I prayed.

Tom stayed with me until I got all the necessary paperwork and decisions made. I got my social security benefit taken care of and the military benefits taken care of, and then he went back to England. I went back to work because I had used all my vacation time, and I had to have my income. I dreaded getting up every day, and I worked for another sixteen months, after which I did finally retire. That was a glorious day for me. It was a goal I had attained…but *alone*.

Since then, I have struggled on many days, and I have had many wonderful days, some not so good, and some just plain bad—but I look at each day as a new day. God has been with me through *every* struggle, and I have learned to lean on him first. Gee, that eliminates so much stress for me! (Like my grandson says, "Well, duh, Grandma!") But every now and then I think I am so strong, I can do it on my own…after all, I'm a big girl, and I can take care of myself! He lets me try, and then he reminds me how much easier it is to let him take care of me.

Life is different now. I can't say I really like it this way, but I know it is only temporary and that one day I will join my sweetheart in heaven. We may not be sweethearts or lovers in heaven, but I know we will be *special friends*. I am looking forward to that day.

18

The Circle of Life
By Lois D.

As my husband, Raymond, lay in pain from widespread cancer, he told me, "I'm ready!" He had no fear of death because as a born-again Christian, he knew where he was going: heaven. It occurred to me that with terminal illness there are many similarities between life and death: both are spiritual journeys. Here are my thoughts nine months following his passing from this life to his new life:

Birth	Death
1. Entrance into world	Entrance into eternity
2. Mother senses the baby is coming	The dying sense death is near
3. Labor pains are relieved by joy	Freedom from pain, joyous new life
4. The mother has nine months to prepare	Often nine months to accept/prepare
5. Seasons have passed, life has changed	Seasons have passed, life has changed
6. At birth, baby goes from darkness to light	The dying often see the light
7. Birth relieves mother's labored breathing	Labored breathing changes to peace
8. Held in parents arms and instantly loved	Loved and held by Heavenly Father
9. There is an awe, a hush as baby is admired	Loved ones in awe, peace is seen
10. Baby's fresh new scent	There is an odor that death is near
11. Birth comes when the time is right	Awaits til loved ones seen, God's time
12. Baby grows slowly in womb	Body gradually declines
13. Baby requires food and diapered	Dying are dependent on care of others

14. Baby cannot speak, but cries and coo

Communication occurs without words

15. New life like a beautiful butterfly out of the cocoon

"Good-bye" for now, but one day we will be transformed and our loved ones will greet us with "Hello"!!

19

My Journey of Survival
By Barbara F.

I thought I would always have my husband by my side. God did not have that in his plans. On March 10, 2000, my husband, Ed, was diagnosed with pancreatic cancer, and I was told he had six months to a year to live. I thought they must be mistaken because I could not live without Ed. We did everything together—I could not imagine my life without him.

Two days later I was hit with another bombshell. Ed had been taken down for a test and I was in the room alone. My husband's doctor came in and said he needed to talk with me. He told me that I needed to get my finances in order because Ed would not be around in three months. After he left I began to cry out to God and ask him why—why me—why Ed had to suffer like he was suffering. I told God that I couldn't handle it. I got no answer from God as to why this was happening.

My husband died two months later on May 11, 2000. As I walked out of his hospital room, I suddenly realized I had lost my mate and my best friend. I felt so empty and alone, even though my three sons were right there with me. That night in my bedroom alone, I realized this was the way it would be for the rest of my life. I couldn't accept that life.

After the funeral I did not want to go back home—it was too empty. A few days later all the family left to go home. What an empty house, and my body felt so empty. I cried, I screamed, I walked the floor, and I asked myself, "What am I going to do?" When I'd get in the shower each day, I would scream at the top of my lungs and say, "God, I can't handle life by myself and I don't want to—why did you take him?" I still got no answers.

At night I could not sleep. I would relive everything that had happened—from the first day Ed got sick, remembering all the days and nights in the hospital—and I would scream out to God, "Please, help me." You can tell by now, I did lots of screaming. I did not want to live. I could hardly wait for daylight, and I hated for nighttime to come. I did not want to cry in front of my children for fear of upsetting them. I began to write in a journal each day. Some days I would write to my husband, and some days I would just write how I was feeling at the moment. That seemed to help. I would not go anywhere; I just wanted to stay in the house. I soon realized that this was not good, but, when I would go out in public and see a husband and wife together, I would get upset and mad and ask God why they could be together when I was alone without my husband.

One night my son and I were in a restaurant and a couple that sat across from us was talking and laughing, and I got so upset we had to leave. I could not handle seeing couples happy and me so sad. I kept asking God why but still got no answers. I could not attend the church we had been in for almost twenty years because I could see Ed everywhere I turned and I would start crying. I decided it was best to leave. I also realized that it was okay to cry in front of my children, and we'd just cry together because they were hurting just like me. I learned crying was a healing process and that it was all right to cry whenever I felt like it.

When nighttime came I would be overcome with fear and I'd scream out for God to please let it all end. Fear was overtaking me, and finally I realized it was Satan who was really taking charge. One morning I lay flat on the floor at the foot of my bed and looked up toward heaven and said, "God, I cannot handle this. I can't live with this fear, and I'm giving it to you." Since that day I have not been afraid.

A few Sundays after my husband's death, I was going down the interstate on my way to church and a couple in the lane next to me were laughing and talking and I got so mad. Then I realized I was being selfish. I thought I should be happy for them and not be upset. A few days later a friend invited me to go to a Bible study with her and I accepted. I thought maybe getting out of the house would help because I was so depressed. That day was the beginning of my journey of accepting my loss.

Through this Bible study I met some wonderful friends, and through the Bible study I was put in touch with Elaine Cook, who was thinking of starting a Widow2Widow™ group. She had lost her husband a few months before I lost my husband, and I thought, if she were strong enough to start this group, I would at least go and see what it is about. I attended the first meeting and my healing began. Being with women who were going through the same thing I was going through and being able to talk to them and know they knew right where I was in my grief helped me to know I could make it with the help of God and wonderful Christian friends.

My husband will be gone five years May 11, 2005, and I have come so far. I still grieve for him and miss him so much, but I've learned God goes before each step I make and he will never leave me. He has not answered my question why and may never here on this earth, but that's all right. I have survived, and I know it is because I put my trust in God and with the help of wonderful friends.

20

The Perfect Cross
By Lois D.

Donald said at his father's funeral that, much like the mechanic mentioned in the book, *The Seven Greatest Men in Heaven,* Raymond Davis was a simple but profound man. Pastor Chester Halstead of Colerain Baptist Church, Kirkwood, Pennsylvania, read Raymond's obituary. He commented, "He was not just a truck driver; he was husband, father, grandfather, and friend."

Raymond Davis left his earthly home and entered his heavenly home on February 29, 2004. He left behind a legacy of love. He now looks forward to his loved ones joining him. This quiet, gentle man bravely fought his battle against cancer. Despite extreme pain, amazingly, he never complained. He was a beautiful example to others during his last months of life. He told people that he was "a winner either way," saying, "If God heals me; I'll be with my family. If I die, I'll be in glorious heaven."

Ray, as he liked to be called, grew up on a farm in southern Lancaster County, Pennsylvania. I moved to Lancaster County at the age of fourteen. I first met Ray riding the school bus to Quarryville Junior High School. Friends in school, Ray and I did not date until after I graduated in 1970. Ray graduated in 1969 and was serving in the U.S. Army when his sister, Bonnie, told me that Raymond wanted me to write to him. I started writing to him while he was stationed in New Jersey. We started dating on the weekends. After four months of dating, Ray had orders to transfer to Fort Stewart, Georgia. We decided to get married on July 10, 1971, because we could not bear being apart.

He left the Army and began working as a diesel mechanic in 1972. The same year, our eldest son, Donald, was born. Karen was born in 1976, and Brian was born in 1979, as I was graduating from nursing school. As our children were growing up, we met our new neighbors, the Rileys. Jay and Denise said they knew that Ray felt comfortable in their new home because he fell asleep during his first visit. They knew that they could trust him because they went to bed, and when they woke up nothing was missing. This was the beginning of a special friendship. Ray and Jay were more like brothers. A couple of years ago, it was discovered that they were really related to each other on Ray's father's side.

Despite both of them moving and the fact that they were no longer neighbors, Ray and Jay were rarely apart. Ray worked in Westchester as a diesel mechanic and would pass the Riley home on the way to and from work. There were very few days that he did not stop by. They spent a great deal of time working on cars and remodeling Jay's home. Ray also grew close to Jay's three little girls. Often, Denise would invite him to eat supper there. He would return home to my greeting, "Here's supper!" I was often puzzled as to why he was not hungry. A quiet man, Ray rarely shared his feelings, but with Jay he could share his frustrations, as well as the joys of life. One of the most cherished memories they shared was hunting and fishing. They always went to the Octorara Lake on the first day of fishing season.

Ray's father and stepmother, who lived in Florida, passed away in 1999. We were able to buy their mobile home from the estate. Plans were made to move to Florida in 2003. Ray and I had often visited his dad in Starke, Florida, where he had retired ten years earlier. Ray knew Interstate 95 so well that he could have driven there in his sleep. He thought nothing of taking a long weekend and driving to see our family and friends in Starke. We always attended his dad's church, Bible Baptist. Over the years, we were blessed with two loving church families. We also maintained a friendship with the Howard family from the Army days at Fort Stewart, Georgia. We would always try to stop to see them on the way to Florida.

We made a decision to move to Florida in early 2003. Our house was sold, and we moved our furniture down to Florida in November 2002, but never completed the move. Within weeks, Ray found out he had widespread terminal cancer. Our family and friends—especially Jay—were in shock. Both our church family in Pennsylvania and the one in Florida showered us with prayers and support. It was difficult to see Ray sick from chemo and in excruciating pain. We did not want to say good-bye, but we could not bear to watch him suffer. He became pain-free at 6:00 PM, February 29, 2004, with all of his family present.

One week later at about 6:00 PM, one of Jay's daughters called out to Jay, Denise, and Jay's mother, Evelyn, saying, "There is an X on our floor!" The Rileys had just completed the building of a new kitchen and installed new tile flooring. Of course, Ray had helped to build it, but he had become too ill to see the final product. When Jay, Denise, and Evelyn went to see the X on the floor, they saw that it really was a perfect cross, shining brightly on the tile. This was not a shadow, and there was no light causing the image! Jay remembered that exactly one week earlier, Ray had gone to his new home in heaven. He knew Ray was telling him that he was okay and to focus on the priorities of life and the cross. Jay took a picture of the cross, which stayed there for about twenty minutes. He wanted proof to show others that might not believe him. This picture has been passed on for many to see and believe.

Yes, Ray was a simple man, but he leaves a legacy that there is hope when we believe in Jesus Christ as savior and lord. Notice that Jesus was not on that cross on Jay's floor. He arose and is alive today! I praise God, because I know that I'll see my beloved husband in heaven again someday!

21

Tea Is the Remedy for Loneliness By Lois D.

I began feeling lonely before my husband died of cancer. During his illness, he lost over fifty pounds. He experienced such excruciating pain that even a hug created more pain. I yearned to hold him close and comfort him, but I knew I could not. Oh, how I missed his touch, and that kiss hello or good-bye.

When he died, I terribly missed his presence, his voice, and everything I loved about him. I felt tremendously lonely in my little apartment by myself. I could not handle the silence, so I would go to my daughter's or son's. I thought a lot about heaven and what it must be like. I wondered was Ray was doing and whether he had seen my parents, his father and stepmother, his sister, aunts, uncles, friends, and cousins already in heaven. I was grateful he was out of pain in his new body.

No amount of television, music, shopping, or reading books helped decrease the loneliness. What helped was the Word of God and how he used two special people, Stan and Rhoda Jackson, to minister to me. Ray and I began renting a small garage apartment attached to their house just after Christmas 2003. His cancer had progressed, and he was in a hospital bed most of the time. They told me I could call on them day or night, and they meant it.

After Ray moved into his new residence in heaven, I returned to work following a leave of absence to care for him. On the evenings I was home, Stan and Rhoda would faithfully invite me over for tea, better known as tea time. Stan always had a joke to tell me to get me to laugh. Stan and Rhoda and I would spend devotion time reading the Bible and in prayer. When I was there, I never felt lonely. They helped me get back on my feet. I felt like a baby being weaned from the bottle when I moved to my own place. Of course, they helped me find the home, helped set it up and hang pictures, and most of all provided me with constant love and prayers. I will be forever grateful for the tea that is the remedy for loneliness.

22

My Story
By Sharon L.

What started out as a good weekend with friends in the Smoky Mountains ended up as the worst nightmare of my life. My husband, Wayne, and I had gone to Gatlinburg for a weekend of relaxation and fellowship with four other couples from our church. After spending two days with them, we told them good-bye. They headed back to Nashville, while we planned to stay one more night. Our lives had been extremely busy and stressful during the past few months, and we needed some time to concentrate on each other.

After a wonderful, stress-free day spent in Gatlinburg, we returned to the condo we had rented for the night to watch a movie and relax in the hot tub. Wayne had had a problem for two or three months with shoulder and arm pain, from what a doctor and a chiropractor had diagnosed as a bulging disc in his neck. So I didn't think much about it when he said that he couldn't get comfortable on the couch. For probably an hour or longer, he moved from the couch, to the floor, to a chair—trying to find a comfortable position. I finally asked him if his shoulder bothered him that much, and then he told me that it wasn't his shoulder. He said, "I feel funny in my chest and across my back. Do you think it could be my heart?"

I work in the clinic of a cardiology office, so I know all the right questions to ask to determine if it could be a heart problem. I asked, "Is there any pain radiating to your jaw, neck, or shoulder? Do you have any sharp pain in the center of your chest? Are you having difficulty breathing? Do you have any numbness or tingling in your left arm or hand?" Wayne answered no to all of those questions.

I asked him if he thought we should find an emergency room, and he said, "No, maybe I just have a bad case of indigestion." To me, that made sense, because he didn't have the classic symptoms of a heart attack, and we both had a little bit of an upset stomach after our dinner.

I went to the refrigerator to get a Coke for Wayne to drink, thinking that might help. That is when I heard him making a choking sound. I ran back to him and saw him with a questioning look of fear on his face. Before I could do anything, it seemed as if his breath was sucked out of him, and his body went into a seizure. Within a few seconds, his body relaxed, and I couldn't get a response from him. My mind panicked as I thought about calling 911 because I couldn't even think of the name of the road we were on or the name of the complex we were in.

As I tried to figure out what to do, I remembered that there was another couple staying two doors down from us, and I knew I needed to get help. After I banged on their door and screamed for help, the man came back with me to Wayne while his wife called 911 and the people who owned the condo. (The owners were friends with one of the couples who had been on our trip.)

I mentioned doing CPR on my husband, but the man said that the paramedics were not very far away and we should wait for them. I was in such a state of shock that I couldn't argue, and, having never administered CPR, I was not sure I could perform it correctly. The paramedics did arrive in less than five minutes and began working on Wayne.

They said it appeared to have been a massive heart attack, so they used the defibrillator to shock his heart, and then started CPR on him. The paramedics worked on him tirelessly all the way to the hospital, about twenty to thirty minutes away. While I was in the ambulance, the driver loaned me his cell phone so I could call my pastor in Nashville and tell him what was going on.

I didn't feel as if I could call my sons at the moment, but I needed to tell someone. We finally arrived at the emergency room, where hospital personnel spent another fifteen minutes or longer trying to revive my husband. A nurse took me to another room, because I didn't think I could watch anymore. She asked questions and tried to calm my nerves. While we waited, the owners of the condo arrived. I was glad to see them, since we had met them the day before and knew they were Christians.

In a couple of minutes, the doctor came in and gently told me that Wayne had not survived. When I said that I should have done CPR, he said that more than likely it would not have helped because the heart attack was so massive. He mentioned that the only heart rhythm they could get was ventricular fibrillation, which is one of the worst rhythms a heart can have. If Wayne had survived, he probably would have suffered severe brain damage.

After I calmed down a little and tried to pull myself together, the nurse asked if I wanted to go to the room where my husband was and spend a few minutes with him. As I sat next to his bed and held his hand, it was so hard to believe that this good-hearted, generous man, my husband of almost thirty-three years, who had brought such joy and happiness to my life, was suddenly snatched away at the age of fifty-three.

We had so much more living to do—grandchildren were being born, we were at a good point in our relationship, and things were beginning to look up financially! Why now? Why so young? Why weren't we given a warning? I realized that my whole world had just been turned upside-down!

After spending some time with Wayne, I knew I needed to call family members. One of my sons had already called the hospital to check on us, after my pastor had gone to his house to tell him that his dad had suffered a heart attack. As I called each person to break the news to them, my heart broke even more as I heard their reactions. I remember thinking, as I heard my grown sons sobbing, that I couldn't "make it better" or "fix it" like I had always been able to when they were little boys. I wished that we were together, so I could wrap my arms around them. It was a helpless feeling.

As I write this sixteen months later, that night is still as vivid as it was then. I have relived that night many times. I also went through several months of feeling guilty for not doing CPR, for not asking Wayne what was wrong earlier that evening, for scolding him that night about not taking better care of himself, for telling him I wanted to go to the doctor when we got back home because I was worried and was tired of him feeling bad, for not recognizing the symptoms of a heart attack, for not saying, "I love you!" before he died, for...I could go on and on, but I did realize after a while that I had to release the "if onlys" and stop punishing myself. Nothing I could do would change things or bring him back.

In spite of all the shock and sadness my family went through, it was evident from the beginning of this horrible experience that God was with me. He sent two Christian couples to help me that night, and one of them took me home with them to stay until friends and family could come and get me. The morning after Wayne's death, I sat on the deck of the home where I had spent the night, and, as I looked out over the Smoky Mountains, I was reminded of the verse in Psalm 121: "I will lift mine eyes unto the hills from whence cometh my help." As I thought of all the wonderful times we had spent in these mountains on family vacations, to celebrate wedding anniversaries, or to have a weekend escape, I realized Wayne had died in a place that he had loved.

God's love continued to surround me when we got back home, as people stepped in to clean my house and prepare food for all the family and friends. It was evident in the more than four hundred people who came to the funeral home for the visitation and in the packed 350-seat church sanctuary where the funeral service was held. His love was expressed in the two hundred and fifty or more sympathy cards, and in the gifts of money that flooded in from family, friends, Sunday school classes, my co-workers, and anonymous givers.

God's love was shown by those who allowed me to grieve at my own pace and to cry when I needed to, no matter where I was. God's care was evident even on desktop calendars that seemed to have messages just for me. One at my house, for October 5 (the day Wayne died) said:

> Time is not measured by the years you live,
>
> But by the deeds you do and the joy that you give.

Another one on my desk at work for October said, "The Lord tears down the proud man's house, but He keeps the widow's boundaries intact" (Proverbs 15:25).

One of my first concerns after Wayne's death was that I would be forced to sell our house where we had lived for twenty years because I would not have enough income to continue the payments. So I felt my work calendar really had a message for me when I read that two weeks later.

God's love was evident when one week after Wayne died, our second grandson was born, reminding our family that life will go on and there will be joy again.

As I looked back over the year before my husband died, I realized what an unusual year it had been and how God had blessed us. We had seen each of our sons play the part of Jesus, one in a community theater production of the musical *Godspell,* and the other in our church Easter program. We had spent time with my sister and her husband and gotten to see all of their children and grandchildren. We'd had a couple of occasions to spend time with other relatives that we had not seen in a long time. Wayne's family reunion (that I was not able to attend because of a prior commitment) had been one of the best ever. Our first grandchild had been born, and Wayne had been able to spend a little over four months being a grandpa, which had changed his whole attitude about life. He had been looking forward to our next grandchild, who was due in October.

We had spent quality time with our sons and daughters-in-law. I could look back and see that we had been very blessed to have had a lot of special family times. We had also had the opportunity to spend some time in our favorite place, the Smoky Mountains. It had been a good year!

Six weeks after my husband's death, a co-worker told me of a woman in her church whose husband had died of a brain tumor the week before. My friend gave me her phone number and address and said that maybe we could help each other. A few weeks later, I called her, and a bond of friendship started.

By January, my new friend had heard of a Grief/Share group that was meeting at a nearby church. We decided to attend the first meeting and see what it was about. God was already going ahead of us, preparing a way to help us. At the first meeting, there were two other new widows whose husbands had died suddenly in October and November. We were all about the same age and had been married for more than thirty years. All of our husbands had been in their fifties when they had died. Even though there were others in the meeting who were experiencing different types of grief, the four of us became a great support group for each other. That bond continues one year later, and we intend to get together on a regular basis and be there for each other whenever we need to talk.

Even though we don't like the reason we were brought together, we feel that God's hand was in it, and we praise him for that. Grief/Share was a very good program that helped us realize we were not going crazy, and that all the emotions we were feeling were normal.

As March drew near, I needed to make a decision about attending the Tennessee Woman's Missionary Union annual get-together in Gatlinburg. I had always attended, but I just didn't think I would be able to go back there less than six months after Wayne's death. It would be too hard to face going back to where he had died. When I looked at the brochure for the get-together, there were conferences on grief and a widows' ministry on the list of conferences to be offered that weekend. I didn't remember those kinds of conferences being offered in the past, so I felt like God was again preparing the way for me. The more I considered going, the more it became evident to me that I needed to go. What better time than this to go back to the place where my nightmare had happened? To go to this kind of inspirational meeting with conferences I needed, and to go with women who were willing to stand by me, hold me up, and cry with me was probably the best way to return.

And I am so glad that I did go! I was surrounded by women from across the state that embraced me, prayed with me, loved me, encouraged me, and told me of all the times they had prayed for me.

The conferences on grief and widows were a great help, and meeting Elaine Cook, who started the Widow2Widow™ ministry, was a blessing. At one of her conferences she shared information about the first widows' retreat, which was to be held in September. At the end of the weekend, I realized that in facing my fears by going to Gatlinburg, I had been rewarded with God's loving care and had received some healing for my broken heart.

I did attend the widows' retreat the following September. The women from my church who had gone to Gatlinburg with me for the get-together had insisted on paying for my registration and fees. The retreat was encouraging, and it brought some more healing to my heart. Listening to the stories of other widows made me realize once again that God hadn't singled me out and that I am not alone in my pain. Hearing women who are further along in their journeys of grief gave me encouragement and hope for my future. I returned home feeling that *I would survive* widowhood and maybe enjoy life again someday.

There are still some very difficult days in my life. Sometimes I feel that if the way I feel now is as good as it is going to get, then I don't know if I'll be able to make it. Other times, when I have had a good day, I feel a flicker of hope. I continue to cling to the verse Jeremiah 29:11: "For I know the plans I have for you, declares the Lord, plans to prosper you and not to harm you, plans to give you hope and a future." I believe that God is in control of my life and will continue to supply my needs. He knows what is in my future, and I have to trust him to reveal his plans for me in his time. God has proven himself to be faithful in my past, and I can trust that he will be faithful in my future.

APPENDIX

Chapter 9:

NIV Encouragement Bible: The Answer for Those Who Hurt
Zondervan Publishing House © 2001
All Rights Reserved

Desiring God: Tenth Anniversary Edition
By John Piper
Multnomah Publishing

Chapter 10:

The Transforming Power of Prayer: Deepening Your Friendship with God
By James Houston
NavPress Publishing Group © 1996
All Rights Reserved

When Will I Stop Hurting? Dealing with a Recent Death
By June Cerza Kolf
Baker Book House Publishers © 2002

When the Crying's Done: A Journey through Widowhood
By Jeannette Kupfermann © 1992
Robson Books
All Rights Reserved

Gayle Haywood: Bible Study
Brentwood Baptist Church, Brentwood, TN

The Grief Recovery Handbook
By John W. James and Russell Friedman
HarperPerennial Publishers © 1998

Facing the Death of Someone You Love
By Elizabeth Elliot
Good News Publishers © 1973

Getting through Grief: Caregiving by Congregations
By Ron Sunderland
Abingdon Press © 1993

978-0-595-35411-5
0-595-35411-4